HOW
TO TEACH
GROUP RIDING

Group riding should always be taught to make fun and laughter a part of every lesson.

HOW TO TEACH GROUP RIDING

Neale Haley

South Brunswick and New York:
A. S. BARNES AND COMPANY
London: THOMAS YOSELOFF LTD

© 1970 by A. S. Barnes and Co., Inc.
Library of Congress Catalogue Card Number: 72-114288

A. S. Barnes and Co., Inc.
Cranbury, New Jersey 08512

Thomas Yoseloff Ltd
108 New Bond Street
London W1Y OQX, England

ISBN 0-498-07593-1
Printed in the United States of America

CONTENTS

With Appreciation   7
Explanatory Note   9

I The Making of a Rider

1. What You Need to Teach Group Riding   13
2. First Lessons   26
3. Trotting Position   45
4. Final Lessons in the Beginner's Ring   59

II The Gaining of Control

5. Dismounting and Mounting   79
6. Control Through Figures and Games   104
7. The Rider Prepares for a Lesson   122
8. Hands and Seats   150

III The Challenge of Perfection

9. Canter   169
10. Beginning Jumping   180
11. Advanced Jumping   197
12. The Skilled Rider   214

IV Ready to Ride Anywhere

13. Happiness with Horses   229
14. Ways to Tackle Fear and Disability   247
15. Safety in the Saddle   256
16. Horse Show   267

Index   281

WITH APPRECIATION

No system of riding is born of one man, nor any book of one author. I am indebted to Marjorie Schaltauer for her ideas on both counts; to Barbara Tornow, who has drawn on her 15 years of teaching this system to offer help and suggestions; to Tom and Linda Kranz, who have both directed camp and headed the riding department, for sharing with me their enthusiasm for this system.

The intermediate section of the book would be less complete without the teaching experience of Doug Haley. Were it not for Kim Haley's ability to express just how it felt to be an advanced rider, the reader would have missed some helpful information on teaching jumping.

Of the many helpers I had in taking pictures, I am especially indebted to Sue Lyet for her painstaking notes. I especially wish to express my gratitude to all who posed at convenient and inconvenient times to help me in expressing an idea in photography. My thanks too, and much love to the horses for their irreplaceable cooperation.

And, without the encouragement of Jacqueline Kranz, there would be no book at all.

EXPLANATORY NOTE

The first three sections of the book are divided into teaching techniques for beginner, intermediate and advanced riders. These techniques may be used if you have only one ring, by so grouping your riders. If you have three rings, as soon as a child has learned the techniques in one section, she is passed into the next ring. Various names can be given to the three rings rather than calling them beginners, intermediate, and advanced. Instructor's ring is often used to take the curse off the beginners' ring. One camp uses Ponies, Prancers, Paddock. Another refers to the riders in the three rings as C's, B's and A's. The advantage of more than one ring is that you have the great incentive of "promotion" to a high ring. This gives children a sense of achievement.

1
THE MAKING OF A RIDER

1

WHAT YOU NEED TO TEACH GROUP RIDING

Teaching riding can give you deep satisfaction, and your students a sense of accomplishment. The swifter the progress of your riders, the greater your pride and theirs. A system of riding is presented here that turns beginners into skilled riders within a few weeks. You need responsive horses, a safe place to ride, and a teacher's desire to help others learn. The desire must be fortified with patience and enthusiasm. Horses will test your patience with their own horse-wisdom; riders will need your enthusiasm to support their doubting hearts. Whether you face the sun of July outdoors, or the chill of January in an indoor ring, you will share with your riders a joy in the horses, the riders' happiness in progress, and the activity that makes riding in a ring, on trail, or in a show, one of the most exciting sports of our day. As a teacher of riding you will share your students' success not for a few short years of an athlete's prime, but for decades and generations.

One of the great truisms is, "if you wish to reach the heart of a child, teach her to ride." One summer at camp, during the first vesper service, a young girl created a sensation by sliding down what was called Suicide Hill when it was slick with mud. The lanterns the campers held illumined the steep ravine as she made her dramatic descent to the words of a hymn that grew fainter each time she fell.

That night the girl told me, "It's no fun being good,

you know, but I have a great time being bad." Yet she, like most rebellious children, responded to the discipline a horse metes out when the child is trying to make him obey. This girl was too inexperienced at first to ride the horse she loved; but her love for the horse became the incentive to make her work for something good, day after day. In the final horse show she rode that horse. The stubborn lines were gone from her face, and her heart was in her eyes when her glance caught mine. The horse had been the channel through which I had reached her.

Horses are the first prerequisite for a successful program. They should be nothing-bothers-me type animals. They must keep calm when their riders lose their balance or their hats. None of them should feel the urge to nip when a rider mounts, nor give a vindictive kick after a rider tightens the girth. Those horses which bolt at butterflies or roll to be rid of their riders must be cured or sold.

When you are buying horses, if your knowledge is scanty, choose a reliable dealer. I remember a good many years ago when my parents were buying horses for their summer camp, a dealer brought a horse "guaranteed safe for children." My parents soon learned that every horse he brought was guaranteed reliable for children, since they were buying horses for children.

The campers named the horse Peanuts because he was the color of peanut butter. The first day at camp, Peanuts became attached to a blackberry bush on the far side of the riding ring. He lowered his head, lay down and rolled. The riding instructors rode him, and he passed the blackberry bush as though it did not exist. If there was a child with poor control on his back, as soon as he reached the blackberry bush, down he went to roll.

So Peanuts went back to the dealer. His replacement was a horse of a lighter color. The first time this horse

What You Need to Teach Group Riding

The horses you own should be the "nothing bothers me" type.

walked around the ring he rolled beside the blackberry bush.

"Peanuts!" the children said. "Peanuts is back."

It was Peanuts, dyed a new color.

No matter what color or breed your horses are, they become more and more important every day, because every day your riders love them more. Each horse in the select group you have chosen should have a gentle spirit, a willing spirit, and, to each of his riders, a personality. If any of your riders, or helpers, or riding assistants, try to show their cleverness by picking out faults in your horses, discourage them. It is simple enough to find faults in a horse. Try to find a horse without one! Your success in teaching riding depends on the confidence your riders have in your horses.

It also means the success of your business. Horses are worth every dollar you invest in them. You may raise thoroughbreds, or have a love for Arabs or saddlebreds or Morgans. The horses of the Vikings, the Iceland ponies, may appeal to you. If you also add a few horses that win in shows, it is all to the good and helps bring in your clientele.

You will need keen judgment in picking your horses, but it is not an impossible task. A gentleman in Greenwich had expert advice in choosing a hunter for his daughter, who wanted to enter shows. He invested $2,000 in a thoroughbred. Week after week his daughter won blue ribbons in jumping classes, and her father took greater and greater pride in her horse. His pride soared, however, the day a man offered to buy the horse for $23,000.

Everyone knows that papers do not make the horse. A horse dealer once showed my mother a sturdy chestnut gelding, marked with white on his legs and face. When Mother failed to exclaim at the beauty of the horse, the dealer turned red and said, "I tell you, if I had papers for this horse, I could get $2,000 for him." He was probably right. Mother paid $350.

If you have a small stable be careful to choose horses quiet enough for beginners . . .

*which will respond with spirit when ridden by an **advanced** rider.*

If yours is a small stable, be particularly careful to choose quiet horses which will respond with spirit when riden by an advanced rider. A horse that is gentle does not need to be dull.

I once knew a horse called Missy, an example of the type of horse small stables need. Missy was usually assigned to the newest and smallest riders. Any advanced rider who was asked to ride Missy felt insulted until the day the owner of the stable chose Missy for herself. "You think Missy is slow?" she asked. "Watch!" A touch of the owner's leg to Missy's side was all it took. Missy leaped away as if acting for a movie scene of an Indian chase.

"You think Missy is difficult to turn?" the woman asked. In an instant Missy was circling barrels so quickly the dust skipped from her heels.

Immediately, everyone wanted to ride Missy.

You not only need gentle horses but a safe place to ride. There are many definitions of a safe place to ride, but, fundamentally, it is a place where you can teach beginners without depending on the skill of the riders to keep the horses under control.

I once taught in a grassy, triangular field that was bordered on one side by a rushing creek and on another by a bank that rose sharply 50 feet above the field. The third end was closed off with log stalls for the horses. It was a pleasant place to teach riding. Somehow horses respect the barriers of nature more than the barriers of men. There were no gates to break, no fences to jump. None of the horses ever tried to run away by splashing through the creek or by scaling the bank.

Trail rides, of course, are one of the greatest assets to any riding program. You do not need to own your own trails; you only need secluded areas in which to ride. After hours of work in the ring, a walk through wooded lanes and grassy meadows puts the spring back into a horse's step and the excitement back in a rider's eyes.

What You Need to Teach Group Riding

Your riding program will be appreciated most for the trail rides you take through secluded areas where vistas from the hilltops lie ahead.

Many years ago, when the gas company put in a pipeline close to the camp property, my parents were quite distressed. The pipeline cut channels up the sides of ravines, rearranged fences through fields for a right-of-way, and was eventually sowed with grass for mile upon mile. The campers viewed the pipeline and begged, "May we take a trail ride up that?" Who would think the gas company had opened vistas from the hill tops for all the horse owners in the countryside?

You need at least one ring for teaching. It is better to have two for this enables you to divide beginners and more experienced riders. If you have a large group, three rings is best of all.

The beginners' ring should have double fences. This is an important safety feature. The inside fence prevents horses from crossing the ring unexpectedly. It also serves

With large groups of riders, three rings are the easiest division for teaching.

The beginners' ring should have double fences.

What You Need to Teach Group Riding

as a guide for the horses, making them easier to control.

The intermediate ring should have a long straight side for trotting. Continuous circles become boring for horses and riders. However, the ring should be small enough to enable an instructor to be heard easily anywhere in the ring.

The advanced ring should be a large paddock with room for several jumps, areas for figure eights, and at least one straight side where cantering can be taught.

With your horses and rings ready, you can turn to the teaching of riding. To be successful you need a tried method of teaching, and—if you can possibly find them—enthusiastic instructors.

The system presented in this book has been tested with several thousand children for more than 20 years. It has been successful in eliminating accidents, the bugaboo of all riding establishments. In fact, in a camp where there were 60 horses and 150 children riding every day, an insurance agent covering the camp was so impressed with the lack of claims that he said, "You could really carry your own insurance. I've never known any camp to have so few accidents." The system is effective whether you have 60 horses, or just one on which you teach your own child.

The stress is on teaching rather than on the horses. Yet, even they are benefited by the system. They are trained as the children learn. The techniques that have been most effective in making skillful riders are the ones illustrated here. They are applicable to riders of all ages.

Usually, riding programs in camps or schools are successful only if a highly qualified teacher is found. Too often those who are hired have little knowledge of how to teach, although they may be qualified riders. This book enables your entire staff to become proficient teachers. The system demands effort on the part of the instructors, a willingness to stand in a ring and teach continuously, even a willingness to run beside trotting horses when a rider needs special assistance. By living up to the demands of teaching, as outlined here, the instructor will have the greatest reward a teacher can ask, *success*.

In fact, if you plan to go into teaching as a career, whether in the riding field or not, you will benefit greatly by working with this system for a few months. Children bring to a riding lesson such an earnest desire to learn that, if your teaching techniques are clear, the children respond with rapid progress. You may well doubt that spending a summer teaching riding will make you a better geography teacher, but once you have experienced the response to this riding system, it will be easier for you to achieve this response in every teaching field.

You will have the most success with this system if you stress the good qualities in the students you teach. Both inside and outside of the ring your teaching brings out the qualities of character that help a student learn. These same qualities also mean happiness for the individual. A willful child, for example, may jerk her horse around so that he obeys her, but until she gives up her willfulness, she cannot develop gentle hands. As you are teaching such a child to be gentle but firm with her touch on the reins, she is gaining self-control.

A discerning teacher is able to pick out the major fault that is preventing a child from progressing. She gives that fault priority over anything else the child is doing wrong. No one learns well by being told only his mistakes. Whatever a rider is doing *right* must be stressed. How fast would a student in arithmetic progress if the teacher only taught that two times two is *not* five?

When I was looking over the progress cards for a group of intermediate riders I had been asked to teach for an hour, the list covered such faults as, "uneven stirrups, elbows out, one rein longer than the other." The riders did make these mistakes, but the major fault was

What You Need to Teach Group Riding 23

lack of control. The first time I let the group trot, three horses nearly ran me down.

A child on a horse concentrates on learning, so the instructor must concentrate on her safety. This means watchfulness.

One summer when I stopped at the pool on my way to the riding ring, I noticed a five-year-old girl standing a single step down at the shallow end. Because I knew she was afraid of the water, her bravery amazed me. When she ventured down another step, she worried me.

"Shouldn't you stop Patty from going any deeper?" I asked the instructor.

"Oh, I can't go in," she said, "I just set my hair."

Suddenly, Patty turned a backward somersault. Her wide eyes stared at me from under the water. I jumped in, riding boots and all, to scoop up Patty. The need for alertness in the riding ring had trained me to act instantly, so that Patty was out of the water before she realized she had been in danger. She did not even cry. A week later she was swimming by herself.

A lifeguard never takes his eyes from the people on the beach. A riding instructor has the more difficult task, because he has to watch both horses and riders. If you see a horse with a wild look in his eye, you know it means trouble. Sometimes your shout, if it is demanding enough, will cause the horse to pause. Horses, just as dogs, do not like to be scolded.

One riding instructor discovered the horses obeyed her more quickly than the children did. If she noticed Thunder with a look that said he was considering rolling in the dirt on a hot day, she would call out, "No, Thunder. No." Every horse in the line would prick his ears as if to say, "Who, me?" Thunder, however, knew he was caught. Up his head would go, forward he would step eagerly to show how good he was.

If the horse you see contemplating a wicked deed begins

to put his thought into action, there is no time to yell to another instructor who is nearer the horse. By the time you explain what is wrong, it will be too late. Run. You can reach the horse in time.

When you are choosing instructors to help you, if you are able to find people with a sense of responsibility, they will also have a sense of safety or be able to develop it in the riding ring. If price tags could be put on the qualities most needed in riding instructors, a safety sense would have the highest tag.

Next in importance is enthusiasm. Your riders will be happier and learn more quickly if your instructors are enthusiastic. Unless an instructor loves people and horses, she cannot bring enthusiasm to her work.

Instructors also need to be willing to follow the system of riding outlined here. Personal preferences should be subjugated in order to keep the teaching uniform. Younger girls, especially those who come to help teach, need to be told that following this system does not mean their way of riding is incorrect. They will have seen a judge in a show pin a rider who has ridden with an unusual style. The judge pinned the rider because of the good results she had with the horse. This system achieves results with horses and children, but the results are many times better if the teaching is uniform. When an advanced level of riding is reached, the more systems a rider investigates, the easier it is to choose the one that works best for her.

Photographs can be a definite aid in teaching riding. Snapshots of your riders, compared with the pictures in this book, will enable your students to see their own faults. This visual evidence often convinces a rider of mistakes she otherwise would not believe she had. When this book is used as a textbook, students take pictures of each other. They quickly develop perceptiveness by comparing their own pictures with those in the text.

In the pages that follow the riders are called children,

What You Need to Teach Group Riding

but the method applies to a beginner of any age. Because the pictures were taken in a girls' camp, most of the children were girls. One aim in taking the pictures was to show the naturalness that characterizes a good rider. The spirit of fun children feel when they are among horses shines through. Many of the pictures were unposed, taken to catch the joy of the moment, the pride a child feels when doing something well, or an unconscious fault.

The happiness that can be yours by teaching riding is here before you. Share the joy a child has when she feels one with her horse because their will is one. Carry this joy with a laugh and smile into your lessons. Between you, the horses, and the system, you must succeed.

2
FIRST LESSONS

The most important ingredient an instructor can bring to his teaching is praise. No matter how large the class, how foolish the questions, how trying the horses or how hot the day, an instructor must keep his smile. It will make him more successful as a teacher than years of riding experience.

One of the best teachers I have ever known was afraid of horses and could not ride herself. Whenever a new instructor gets that look of panic in her eyes when, for the first time, she views a class of 20 beginners in a ring, someone tells her about Anne. Anne was a good imitator so that she followed the riding system correctly, but her success was due to her perpetual smile.

The riding system, in the beginners' ring, is aided not only by the double fences but by the use of a lead horse. The lead is ridden by an experienced rider, preferably an instructor, though an advanced rider is often able to obey instructions carefully enough to lead.

Behind the lead horse, the other horses are put in line in an order in which they work well, and they are never permitted to pass. Whatever gait the lead horse takes, the other horses, being follow-the-leader type animals, take, too. Since the lead rider obeys the instructor's signals, the instructor in the center of the ring has control of the entire class. The system has been proven to be a very safe one.

First Lessons

Even the horses learn the routine of working in line. Peggy, a horse who had always been used in the beginners' ring, could be trusted with any child. Once she was discovered trotting exactly the proper distance from the horse in front of her, and she stopped when the others stopped, although her rider had dropped both reins. Another time, Peggy walked into her place in line ready to begin the lesson even though her rider had failed to come.

Children always arrive at their first lesson bubbling with enthusiasm. Most of them have watched Olympic jumpers on TV and imagine themselves winning before cheering throngs. Success shines in their eyes. As a girl approaches the horse you have chosen for her, her first doubts bud. The saddle looks miles high. At this point it is a waste of effort to try to teach her how to mount correctly. Show her at the end of the lesson, after she is familiar with the horse and has more confidence and balance.

It is much easier to begin where her mental "set" is, on the horse. A word about which foot to put in the stirrup and where to grab the saddle will be enough to get most girls mounted. Others need a boost by the seat of the pants.

Now that the child is on the horse, she can hardly wait to be shown what to do. Her hands will be fumbling for the reins faster than you can show her how to hold them. The next few moments, while she is getting the kind of individual attention that is rare in a large group, are precious. Her blank look is similar, no doubt, to the one you wore the first time you sat in the driver's seat while someone explained the clutch, brake, power steering, ignition and gear shift. You know that only by practicing how to control her horse will she really understand what you say. Even so, you go through the routine.

She pulls on the reins to stop. One rein means turn.

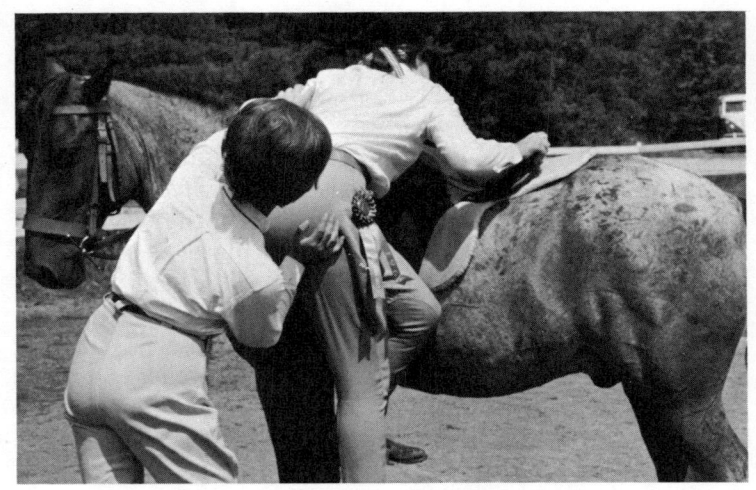

An explanation on how to mount will enable most of your riders to do it. Others may need a boost.

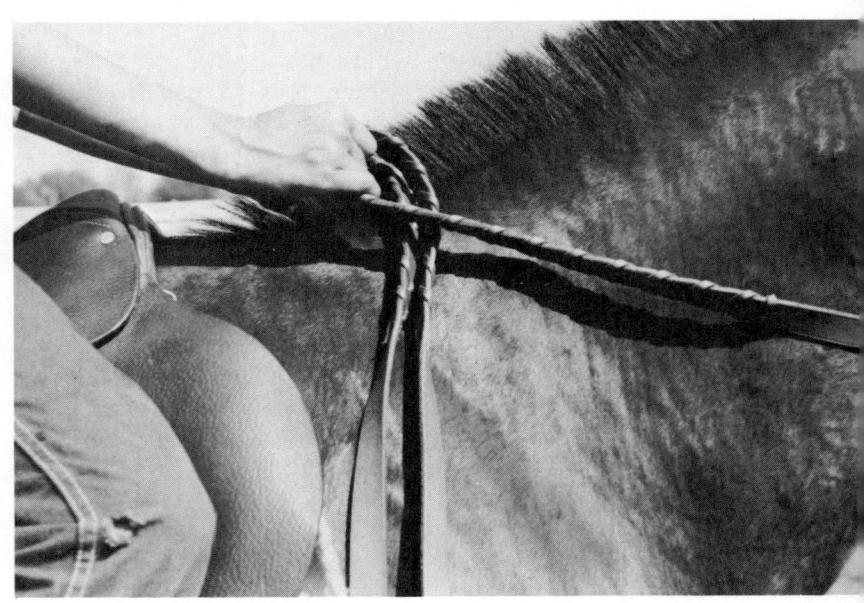

Show the rider how to hold her hands.

She pulls both reins to stop.

A nudge with her heels, but *not a kick*, will ask her horse to go. As a final precaution, you give a firm, downward pull on her heel. Though you have said the same words a hundred times to a hundred children, that glint of excitement in this child's eyes makes it worth saying it all again.

All you need to do is look at a class of beginners who have mounted horses for the first time and you will want to shout, "Everyone hang onto the mane." It is such a handy safety belt. I much prefer a grip on the mane to a grip on the tree of the saddle or to seeing

One rein means turn.

A nudge with her heel, but not a kick, will ask her horse to go.

As a final precaution, before the rider walks, give a firm, downward tug on her heel.

First Lessons

a child slip precariously to one side at the first tense moment. It is actually difficult sometimes to convince a child that she will not hurt a horse by pulling his mane. Before a child begins to walk her horse, she should know you do not mind if she catches hold of the mane.

One of the most tense moments for an instructor is when she gives the command for the class to walk. This is not due to lack of confidence in the lead horse and rider, or fear that one of the horses will stumble, but due to all those unpredictable children. Beginners seem to have an inner determination to stay on their horses, however, for in 20 years of teaching I do not remember a child ever falling off the first time around the ring.

Actually, the major problem that plagues you is the horses' sociability. They keep getting closer and closer to their barnmates. If the riders could only learn by magic how to keep just enough tension on the reins at just the right moments, the distances between horses would stay perfect. Before the horses begin to bunch up in line is the time to have each child look over her horse's ears and try to see the heels of the horse in front of her. As long as the rider is able to see those heels, her horse is not close enough to be kicked. By keeping the correct distance apart, the riders will not make kickers out of good horses.

The children will get their first experiences stopping their horses while they are learning to keep the correct distances in line.

One of the most important lessons in safety should be taught at this point: to obey the command, "ALL STOP." This is an emergency command. It means every horse in every ring stops immediately. A horse that is rushing off always feels foolish when all the other horses suddenly stand still, and he will usually stop, too. Often you see trouble before it starts, a dropped rein, a child slipping off. The call, "ALL STOP" can prevent an accident. There

Proper distance can be enforced if each rider is able to see the heels of the horse in front of her. The lead rider watches that this distance is always maintained.

In every class there is always one child who will try to stop her horse by lifting her hands chest high.

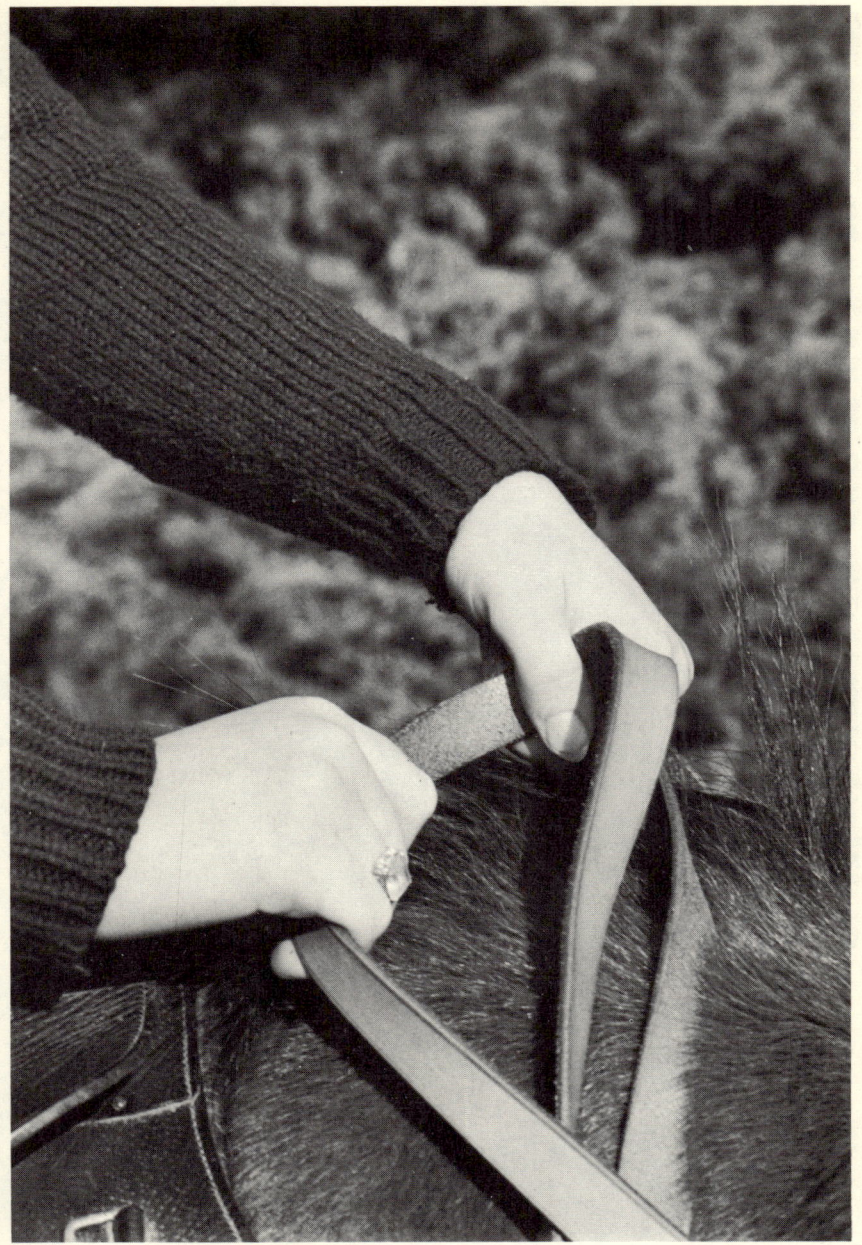

She needs to shorten her reins, (1) by taking the end of her right rein in her left hand . . .

(2) by sliding her right hand along the rein toward her horse's mouth . . .

(3) by letting go of the end of the right rein she held in her left hand. Then she shortens the other rein.

should be frequent rehearsals of the command when there is no emergency, just as a school has fire drills.

In every class of beginners there seems to be one child who will try to stop her horse by sticking out her

Beginners often hold their hands upside down on the reins.

First Lessons

elbows and lifting her hands chest high. The old saying that a rider follows her hands up and off a horse may not be proven, but hands in the air usually do indicate a child is off-balance. That scares any instructor. High hands also fail to stop a horse. The best cure is to teach a child to pull the reins toward her stomach.

Because high hands are accompanied by long reins, the child also needs to know how to shorten her reins. In order to shorten the right rein, for example, a child should take the end of the right rein in her left hand between her thumb and finger. This frees her right hand to slide along the rein toward her horse's mouth. She should then be reminded to let go of the end of the right rein.

More often than not the child who has long reins is also holding her hands upside down as if she were shaking hands with the reins. Though an inexperienced instructor tends to think such a child is going to be difficult to teach, this is not always true. There is so much excitement and tension for a child, when she first rides, that she often listens but does not hear. Most children who are handed the reins will turn their hands upside down to take them. For some reason this seems natural to them. Too many Westerns on television, perhaps.

The child you worry about is the one who persistently holds her hands the wrong way. A simple method of correction begins by taking the reins out of her hands entirely. Have her hold her hands, palms down, over the horse's withers, then touch the tips of her third fingers together.

While you hold the reins, have her rest her hands on top of them and close her fingers.

When she turns her thumbs up, she will be holding her hands right side up.

Last, the bight of each rein must be flipped over her fingers and her thumbs placed on top of each rein. The

There is a simple method of correction. Have the child touch the tips of her third fingers together while she holds her hands over the horse's withers.

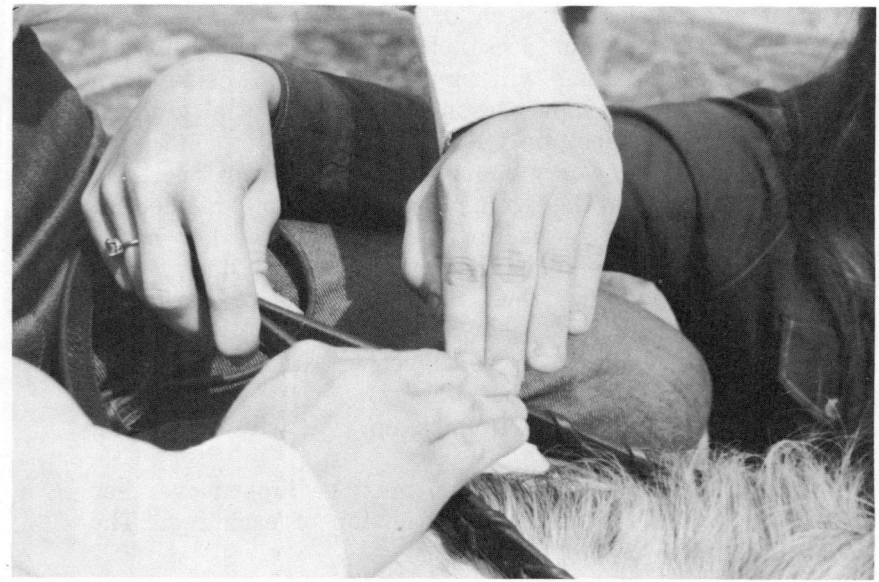

Pull both reins back so you are holding the horse. Her hands come down on the reins.

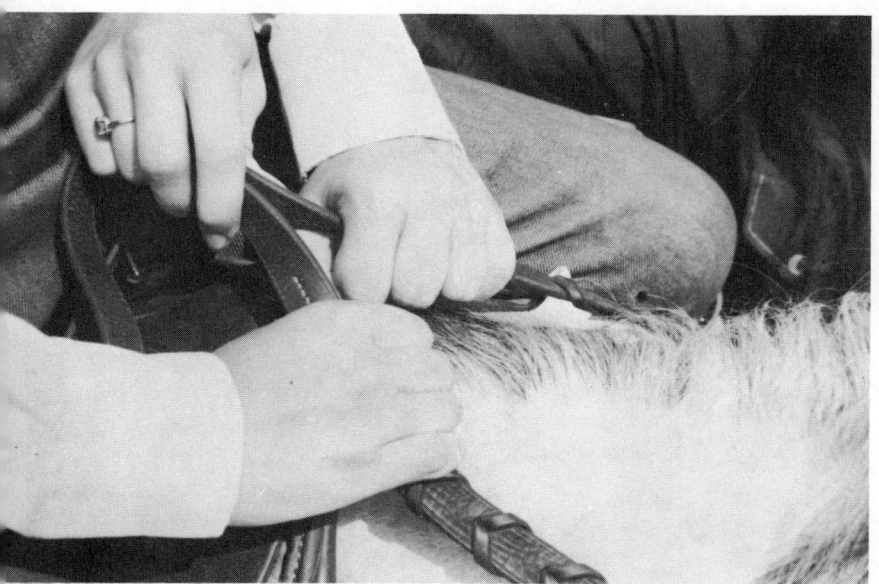

She closes her fingers around the reins.

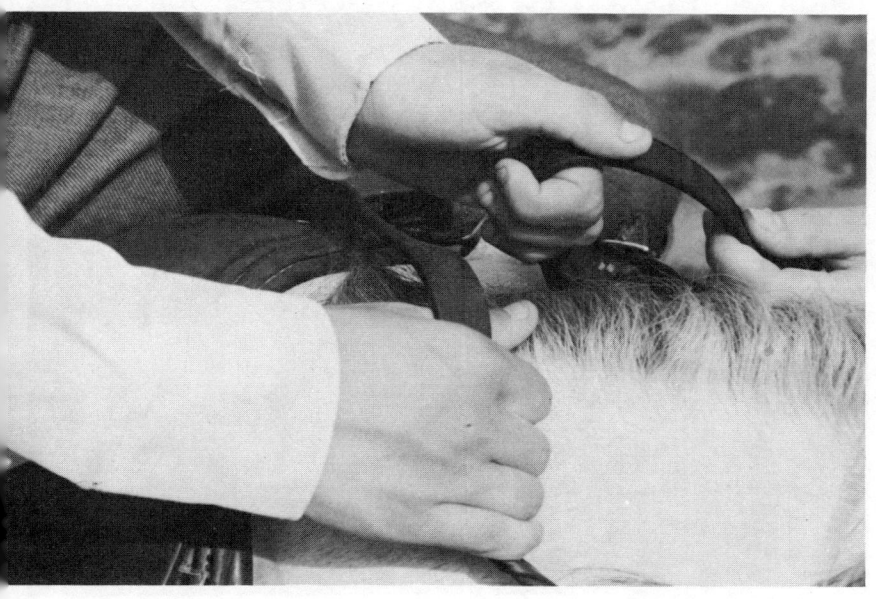

The end of each rein must be flipped over her fingers and her thumb placed on top of it.

Beginners often let the ends of the reins stick out awkwardly from their hands.

First Lessons

last step is the most difficult to make children understand. They fumble with and twist the ends of the reins. You soon find yourself spotting beginners by noting reins standing up like two sticks from the middle of a child's palms.

The other problem that worries an instructor is feet that have been shoved too far into the stirrups. I remember vividly being told of the first time my three year old daughter was allowed to canter on an English saddle. The child's foot had slipped home in the stirrup, she had slid off and would have been dragged if she had been big enough. Instead, she swung by one leg under the horse's belly. Her screams and swinging body made the horse bolt around the ring. The instructor, full of courage, caught the horse. The child was unhurt. As soon as she was on top of the saddle she wanted to canter again.

You need to show a child where the ball of her foot is. She cannot keep her heel down unless the ball of her foot is on the stirrup.

If children are taught to keep their weight in their stirrups while they are learning to ride, their feet will not slip too far into the stirrups. You often need to show a child where the ball of her foot is. She cannot keep her heel down unless the ball of her foot is on the stirrup.

The eagerness that urges children to try as hard as they can to do what you ask during the first lessons always pleases an instructor. Anyone who has tried to teach uninterested children in school finds a special thrill in working with beginning riders. Some instructors so enjoy the success they achieve in the beginners' ring they want to spend all their time there.

Keep building higher on the bridge of their enthusiasm, and the children will be posting so quickly they will hardly seem the same children you helped to mount the first day.

3

TROTTING POSITION

The trotting position has many names. Children have been told it is the half seat, the jumping position or the galloping position. I use "trotting position" with beginners because children grow pale at mention of the synonyms. What it really means is a standing position in the saddle in which the rider is balanced no matter what the horse is doing. A firm trotting position is a basic building block a child needs to become a rider. She will even use this position when she learns to jump. It will always be natural to her if she learns it her first day on a horse.

Actually, it is one of the easiest riding techniques to teach. The first step, shortening the reins, must be emphasized. It is the tool of control. If a child loses her balance while she is standing, the short reins automatically stop the horse. There is no time to shorten reins once the child starts to slip.

Earlier in the lesson you told the child she could hold the mane. Now she must hold the mane. Along with each rein she takes a bit of the mane about halfway up the horse's neck. Be sure she keeps one rein in each hand, not reins in one hand and a bit of mane in the other. She needs those reins to turn and stop. She also needs the mane, while she is standing, to help her keep her balance when the horse trots. Because she is holding the mane, she will not tug on the horse's mouth with each step. Her hands should be close together on the

The trotting position is a standing position in the saddle in which the rider is balanced no matter what the horse is doing.

mane. Otherwise, when she no longer needs to hold the mane, she is likely to hold one hand in front of the other.

As soon as the rider's reins are correct, she may stand in her stirrups. Her knees should be bent slightly; her heels down and her weight on the stirrups. Her shoulders will be further forward than her buttocks. She should have her head up and be looking between her horse's ears. The position is similar to the one she would take if she were standing on the ground ready to jump over a log without making a running approach.

By teaching the trotting position during the first lesson, you will be able to have your group of riders trot the first day. This position is the only safe way for inexperienced riders to trot. The advantages of trotting the first day are great. The deep fear of falling off if a horse moves quickly, as well as the fear of being unable to

Trotting Position 47

stop him, are proved groundless. Every child's confidence soars after she trots once. Thereafter, each lesson is easier and more fun.

For some reason, a beginning class always looks hopeless before the riders learn the trotting position. When you have just enough time left in the first lesson to teach it

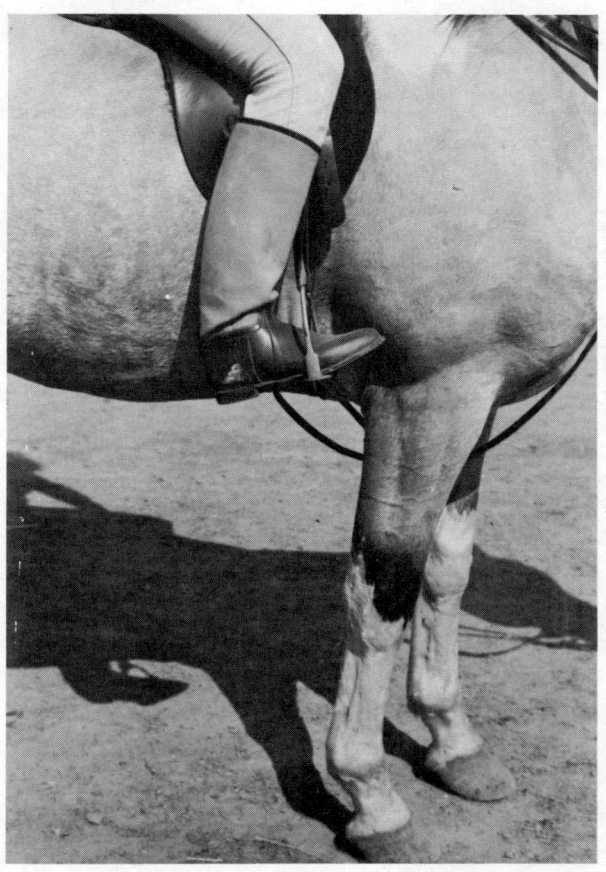

Her knees should be bent slightly, her heels down and her weight on the stirrups.

The trotting position is similar to the stance she would take if she were standing in the woods ready to jump over a log.

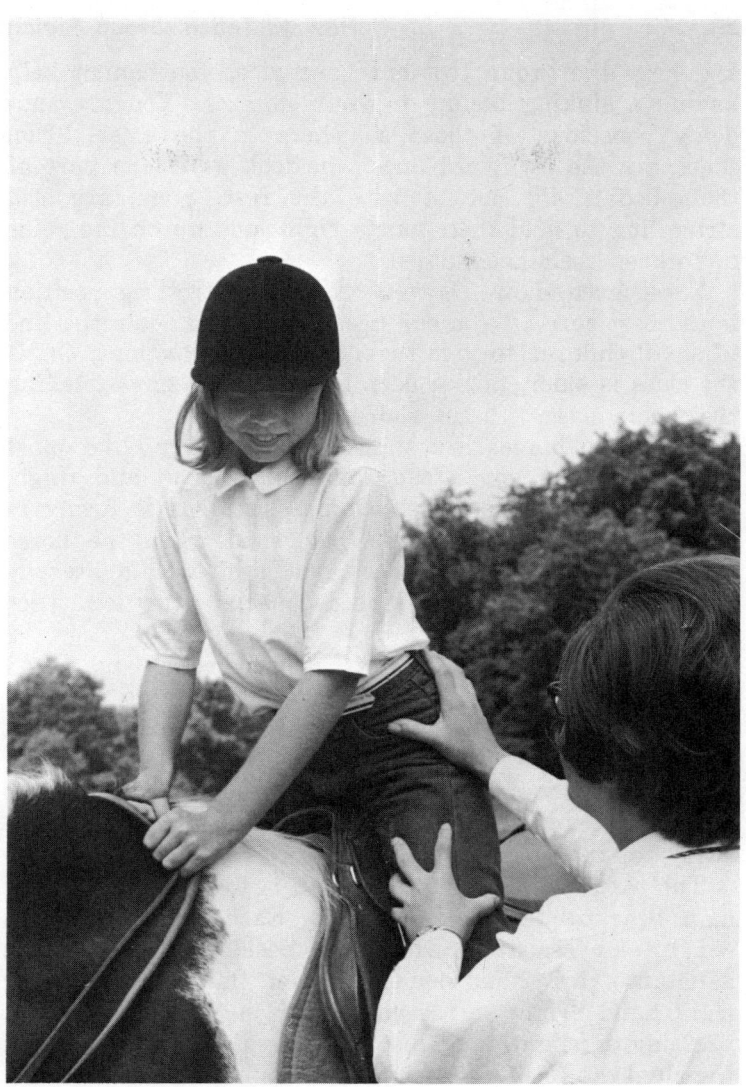

Grasp each child's thigh to make sure she is firmly in place and will not topple backward when her horse takes a step.

and have the group trot once or twice, you cannot help having a sinking feeling in your stomach. You are suddenly conscious of those slouchers in the class. Then there are the awkward ones who look as if one part of their bodies did not fit with the rest. Some are still struggling to hold their hands right side up on the reins or to keep their heels down.

Experience shows, however, that the trotting position is the best cure-all you can use. Bravely go down the line of small children to give them specific instructions. Or, if the class is older, take a deep breath and begin by telling the whole class, "Please shorten your reins."

While the horses are standing still, every child must be checked. As you grasp each child's arm and thigh, tug her backward a little to make sure she is firmly in place and unlikely to topple backward when the horse takes a step. If, as you check, you find a child literally shaking in her boots, she needs special attention. (See Chapter 14.)

When the class is able to shorten reins and stand easily, the group should practice the trotting position at a walk. Usually two or three circles around the ring, interspersed with stopping, resting, standing and walking again, are enough to prove to the riders how simple it is to stand up when a horse is moving. Then they are ready to trot.

The safe way to have them trot is to take four horses at a time behind the lead horse. Each horse should be led by an assistant who runs beside the child. The assistant's left hand should be on the reins and her right hand firmly on the child's leg just below the knee, pressing it slightly against the horse. This touch gives the child the feeling of being "held on" but does not interfere with her movement, since her lower leg must remain still whether it is held or not. Sometimes the rider has perfect control so that the assistant only needs to keep

Trotting Position 51

You will be more confident about a class if each horse is led the first time your riders trot.

a grip on the rider's leg. With older girls the assistant may run along in case she is needed and to give the children confidence, but she does not need to touch either horse or rider. Your helpers may be girls who are fence-sitters and horse-lovers, friends of the riders or paid assistants. Whoever the helpers are, they will lose pounds the first week they run beside beginning riders.

With each group of beginners who are learning to trot, no matter what the age, the lead horse must be used. The greater the skill of the riders, the sooner the assistants can stop running beside the horses and the larger the group of horses which trots each time. Within two or three lessons most of the riders should be trotting alone.

Once in a while you have a natural rider, a girl who does everything right the first time. Annie was such a child. Although she was assigned to one of the more stubborn horses for her first lesson, she listened to the instructions on how to dig a heel into her horse, and after the first kick, he walked immediately for her every time she asked. Her trotting position was secure the moment she stood in her stirrups. One of the young assistants who was running beside Annie explained the way to post. So Annie posted, perfectly, during her first lesson. It was difficult to tell who was more excited, Annie or the riding assistant.

Most children, however, must go through the process of learning the trotting position first. While a child is standing in her stirrups, she does not feel the bounce of the horse's trot, so that she is able to concentrate on her position.

The first fault you will probably notice is heels up in the air. If a child's heel goes up, her toe slips into the stirrup. Sometimes the fault is not her own. Stirrups that felt comfortable at a walk are too long for her when she trots. When you are adjusting stirrups, however, it is better to err on the side of long stirrups than of short ones, which make a child look and feel like a jockey.

If a child complains that she cannot put her heels down because her ankles will not bend, and if when you try to force her heel down, you discover she is right, there is a cure. She can practice flexing her ankles while she is sitting on a bench, or every night at the dinner table. In time, riding, itself, will train her ankles to flex, but she can speed the process.

An experienced horsewoman once told me that practicing riding off a horse had helped develop her skill. Although she rode every day as a child, she used to sit on a chair in her bedroom and practice riding two hours every day.

Posture, so important to the way a child looks on a horse, can be practiced outside of class, too. A straight back will give a woman an A posture rating, but rare is the woman who has one. Most girls have an arch to

A rider can practice flexing her ankles while she sits on a bench or even while eating dinner.

The arch in a rider's back is often accentuated when she rides.

Correct her by laying your arm up her back, your elbow against her seat, your hand gripping her shirt.

their backs. This arch is often accentuated when a girl rides. You could probably carry a board around with you to lay against arched backs, but the first time you set it down a horse would no doubt step on it. Your arm against a child's back can give her the feeling of a board. Grasp her shirt to hold her shoulders in place, then push your elbow against her buttocks. A pointed finger in her stomach helps her to tighten her stomach muscles.

The huncher is another rider you can help and even make laugh in the process. This girl bends close to her horse's neck as if by bringing her head closer to the ground she has less distance to fall. She will realize the way to stand erect if you lift a bit of her hair as if she were a puppet on a string. When she is trotting, she has to remember to pretend those strands of hair are still being pulled.

Children who have trouble with balance keep falling back on the saddle. Usually their legs have slipped forward. Sometimes it helps to tell them to move forward in the saddle so that their bodies are over their legs. Show them again where their legs should be while they are sitting down. When a rider looks over her knee, she should be able to see the tip of her boot, not her whole foot. When she stands up, her legs should not move at all. While a child is standing, swing her legs forward slowly. She will be forced to sit down. This helps her *feel* what she has been doing wrong. Most children who know their mistakes are able to correct them.

Corrections should always be made in the spirit of fun. If you use these methods as a punishment, you defeat the effectiveness of what you say. Almost all children learn more quickly through praise than criticism. Sometimes, after the fifth class in a day, you are tempted to be short when you correct a fault. Then is the time to remind yourself that riding is the most important thing in that child's life at the moment. Some day, though you

The rider who bends too close to her horse can be corrected in fun as if she were a puppet lifted by the strands of her hair to keep her upright.

The rider whose legs slip forward has trouble keeping her balance when she tries to stand.

may not remember her, this child really may ride on the Olympic team. The way you talk to her the first day she is on a horse may make her a show rider or a failure. The look in her eyes will tell you if you bit your tongue hard enough.

4
FINAL LESSONS IN THE BEGINNERS' RING

The final lessons in the beginners' ring build on the techniques a rider has learned already. The first day in class everyone learned how to stop a horse. Before leaving this first ring, however, a rider should be able to stop her horse even when no one else stops. This is one of her first steps away from dependence on line work and a lead horse. Beginning at the end of the line, have each child stop her horse while the rest of the horses keep moving away. This gives the instructor a chance to see if everyone knows how to stop her horse correctly.

Every day the class has been mounting and dismounting, usually with help from the instructors. The riders also need to learn the emergency dismount in the beginners' ring. The emergency dismount is taught for those rare times when it is safer to jump off a horse than to stay on him. By learning how to jump off a horse, children lose some of their fear of falling off. Each step of the emergency dismount should be so drilled into riders that they remember automatically what to do.

The first important step is to get the riders' feet out of the stirrups. Nothing could be worse in an emergency than jumping off a horse with your feet still in the stirrups.

Next, each child hugs her horse around his neck with both arms. She should not let go of the reins nor take time to shorten them.

Finally, she jumps to the ground, landing on both feet facing the front of her horse. She should hang onto the horse's neck with her right arm to break the force of her jump. Her elbow will still be across his neck when she lands.

The horses should be standing still the first time you teach a class the emergency dismount. There will be much squirming and sliding as the riders wiggle to get off their saddles. Soon, however, the call, "Emergency dismount, NOW," will result in dangling stirrups and laughing voices. In the beginners' ring, you practice the emergency dismount only at a walk.

You are eager to let your riders practice trotting more and more of the time as they learn balance and have greater endurance. One afternoon when I was waiting to teach a class, I became distressed because a riding assistant was permitting an advanced class to canter the entire hour. When I suggested to her this was not wise, she said, "But how much should I work the horses?"

This is not an easy question to answer. Horses are work animals with great endurance, and children are light burdens. If your horses are well fed, have a day of rest every week, and are not overworked in classes, they will work willingly for years. Usually, a 50–50 division of work and walking is a fair system. Of course, if your horses are only working an hour a day, that hour can be strenuous. In every class, however, even if the horses have been ridden before the class and will be ridden after it, the horses should walk the first and last five minutes of the period. Only by sticking to this rule will your riders realize the importance of walking a horse at the beginning of a ride after he has come from his stall, and of bringing him in cool at the end of a ride.

The class will be more interesting to the riders if work and rest are mingled in varying degrees. When the group first learns to trot, you will only trot up one side of the

The most important step in the emergency dismount is to get the rider's feet out of her stirrups.

ring, and walk on the other side, thereby giving the riders a chance to regain their equilibrium. You may let them trot five or six times around the ring at one time, however, when they are learning to post. You might trot only two or three times in an hour if you have "long trots." In between you let the riders walk without stirrups, work

Next she puts both arms around her horse's neck.

Final Lessons in the Beginner's Ring

She swings off the saddle and lands facing the front of her horse.

The rider should begin to post as soon as she is balanced in her trotting position when the horse is trotting, starting or stopping.

The riders hold the manes while they are learning to post.

Final Lessons in the Beginner's Ring

on positions, or practice emergency dismounts. These in between times are the best ones for teaching because the class is listening to you, not to the beat of trotting hoofs.

The trotting position, on which the class has worked so hard, is only the preliminary to posting. Posting is the last technique taught in the beginner's ring.

A child is ready to post when she is secure in her trotting position while the horse is moving, when he starts to trot and when he stops. The last is the most important. Occasionally, a rider feels the rhythm of the trot and seems to swing with it almost at once. Most children need two or more lessons. A few take weeks. This last group should not feel discouraged. By the time they are in the advanced ring they may well be superior riders to the ones who learned to post in two lessons. The learning process is always made up of progress and plateaus.

Posting is simply standing up and sitting down in time with a horse's trotting steps. A child who is ready to post should stand still with her horse. Have her post several times. Let her practice at a walk. It also helps to have her stand on the ground, her feet apart, her knees bent, and squat and stand, squat and stand. This shows her how simple it is to go up and down with her legs still and her back straight.

Children should continue to hold the mane when they learn to post. This prevents them from jerking on the bit. Point out that their elbows bend and straighten each time they go up and down.

The child should stand in her trotting position when she makes her horse trot, then sit down to post. It is much easier to sit down to the saddle than to try to stand up from it. Also, because the child is used to the standing position, she does not feel the need to relax into the saddle and take a double bounce before she can get herself up again.

The moment she posts correctly, tell her, "That's right, keep it up." She cannot know for herself the first time, but your words, coupled with the sensation of rhythm, will show her how it feels to post correctly. Continue to tell her when she is correct until she knows for herself.

There are many ways to help a child who is unable to post in rhythm. She can watch one of the horse's shoulders and try to sit down every time his shoulder is back. She can try counting with you, "One, two, one, two," in rhythm with the horse's steps. Sometimes it helps to let her sit the trot and feel her horse push her up.

A child who posts too quickly may feel the rhythm of the trot if you switch her to a pony, because he takes quicker steps. On the other hand, a child who is a bit "slow-motion" in her posting often gets the feel of the trot if you put her on a large horse with a long stride. The child who posts every other beat should not be corrected until she has a sense of rhythm. Usually, just changing the horses she rides will correct the trouble.

Sometimes you own a horse that has the magic trot for posting. My parents once bought a horse called Flying Cloud, a large palomino, fabled to be a challenging ride for advanced riders. The first week in camp, Flying Cloud ended up in the beginners' ring. Any child who rode Flying Cloud suddenly posted perfectly no matter how much trouble she had had on other horses. If a child was learning to post, she was assured of doing it correctly her first day if she could ride Flying Cloud.

Once in a while, a child forgets everything you have taught her as soon as she tries to post. Quickly put her back in trotting position for another day or two.

A child who tries earnestly to post without success may need a helping boost. Mount her on a small horse or pony whose back you can easily reach. Run beside her horse, and lift her up and down by the seat of her pants.

One summer, a small boy, who was the son of one

Final Lessons in the Beginner's Ring

of the counsellors at camp, tried to post for weeks. His mother often came to the ring, but even her encouragement did not help. He liked to ride Buenos, a large pony who was both quiet and willing. One day, while his

A child who cannot feel the rhythm of posting may only learn how if you run beside the horse and lift her up and down by the seat of her pants.

mother led Buenos to keep the pony trotting, I lifted the boy up and down by the seat of his pants. The boy was silent, as he always was with everyone except his mother, but he kept watching me. Undaunted by those staring eyes, I chatted away about how to post as if he were besieging me with questions. When my breath gave out all I did was lift and lift.

Suddenly, at the end of a half hour, he posted in rhythm four times in a row all by himself. In a couple more lessons, he could post all the way around the ring. His posting was a triumph that made me want to shout. Nor was that all. He began to talk to me. I had a new friend.

Even after children learn to post, their troubles are not over. They develop faults. One of the worst faults is "pumping." A child's shoulders go up and down as if she were working a pump handle.

Small children will "pump" their shoulders unless you change the position of their hands on the mane. In a trotting position, a small child can easily reach up the horse's neck. However, if she sits down with her hands part way up the neck, she has to stretch to keep her hold. Before she begins posting, shift her hands close to the front of the saddle, but be sure she continues to hold the mane. Very little girls may need to hold the saddle itself.

Pumping is almost always caused by the wrong position of the hands. Occasionally, however, a child will pump because she is arching or is simply trying too hard and making work out of posting. Have such a child take her trotting position, her shoulders up straight, and poke her gently in the tummy to show her she should neither arch nor stick her stomach forward in an effort to get herself out of the saddle. Point out that the horse helps the rider to post by thrusting her upward with each trotting step.

Often legs start swinging when riders start posting. Run beside the child with swinging legs and hold one

Final Lessons in the Beginner's Ring

"Pumping" is a mistake that must be corrected early. A small child is able to reach the horse's neck in a trotting position . . .

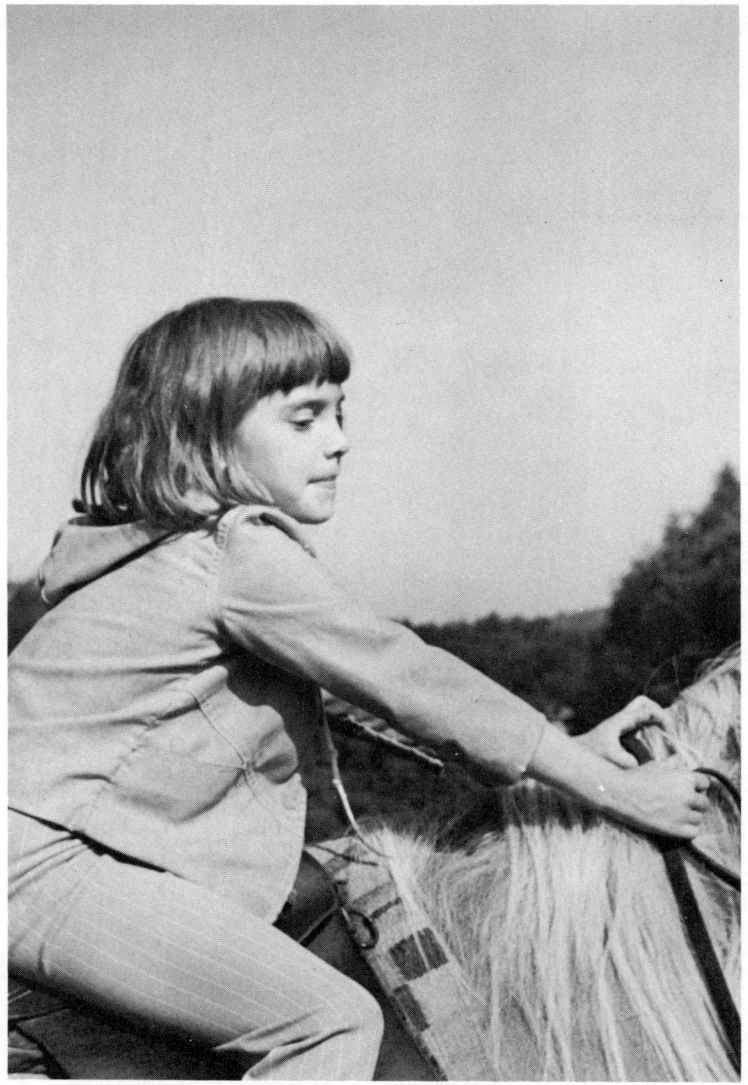

but, when she tries to post, she has to lean too far forward because her arms are so short.

Final Lessons in the Beginner's Ring

Shift her hands close to the saddle while she is in her trotting position . . .

so that she can sit erect in her saddle when she sits down to post.

of her legs still while she trots. She will feel what she is doing wrong, though it may take her a few lessons to correct it.

A child may point her toes at right angles to her horse when she trots. Demonstrate with your own feet what she is doing, so she can correct herself.

You should also correct the child who is leaning too far forward when she is posting.

The next step in learning is to post without holding the mane. Explain to the riders that they must not use the reins to help them post because this pulls on the horses' bits. Have everyone ride with a little slack in her

A child may point her toes at right angles to her horse when she trots, which keeps her from being secure in the saddle.

Correct the child who leans over her horse's neck when she posts.

A rider is cruel who uses the reins to rise from the saddle.

Final Lessons in the Beginner's Ring

reins to discourage using the reins as handles. When the class trots, watch carefully for rein-pullers.

If a child does pull on the reins, have her stop her horse. While you hold her horse, have her drop her reins and post a couple of times. If she has trouble standing without the reins, she will realize she was using her horse's mouth for leverage. No child willingly hurts her horse.

Sometimes a child's hands ride up and down as her body goes up and down. She may be forgetting to straighten her elbows. As a reminder to keep her hands still, she can hold a wisp of mane close to the saddle. The tug of the wisp of mane warns her that her hands are trying to go up in the air.

One day while I was watching a riding exhibition, a tanned, black-haired girl edged up beside me. After we had discussed the riders for a few minutes, she took a deep breath and asked, "Is there any way to keep your hands from going up and down when you post?" She sighed. "I have so much trouble with mine." A look of relief came over her face when I told her about the wisp of mane.

As soon as a rider posts in rhythm on any horse she rides, she is ready to leave the beginners' ring. If you have kept your temper and remembered to laugh often, your beginning riders will always remember you. Every so often in the weeks that follow, you will glance at the other rings and see how rapidly your riders are progressing. It will make you proud.

II
THE GAINING OF CONTROL

5

DISMOUNTING AND MOUNTING

The second ring, the one for intermediate riders, is the ring of control. The lessons taught there are rich with time for practice. The rewards for practice are supple muscles and balance in the saddle. You fill the hours with ideas and games which teach control of the horse and control of the rider's movements until your riders acquire a polished look.

The problem with teaching large groups of children is how to split them among the various rings. The second ring is really an extension of the beginners' ring rather than an adjunct of the advanced ring. Plan to include about half your riders in the beginners' and intermediate rings. The other half use the advanced ring. This division is a means of reward for progress that is most encouraging to your riders. Also, because a child is promoted to the advanced ring as soon as she has control of her horse, she is given the greatest opportunity to practice this control in the larger ring, where she compares herself with the best riders. You may need to divide your advanced riders into groups as well.

Intermediate riders need to learn exactness in handling a horse, as it is the basis of control. In the second ring, the instructor not only insists that a child get the correct response from a horse, but that she does it in exactly the right way from the time she comes into the ring until she leaves it.

Two of the most exacting techniques in a riding ring are mounting and dismounting. They help a child to control her own movements on a horse. You have taught everyone how to get on and off a horse, in a simplified way, in the beginners' ring. There, the instructor gave a boost or lengthened a stirrup if it was needed. Now, the group has moved into the "do-it-yourself" class.

It is easier to teach a class how to dismount than to mount. By teaching dismounting first, you are covering many points that are similar for mounting, only you are teaching them under simpler conditions. Also, the riders begin from a balanced position on top of their horses instead of on the ground, facing the need to reach that point of balance.

The first step in dismounting is one of control. A rider must take both reins crossed through her left hand so that a tug with her baby fingers pulls the left rein, and a tug with her second finger puts pressure on the right rein. To teach a class how to take their reins in this manner, have each rider hold her left hand above her right hand without changing her normal grip on either rein. The children next rest their left hands on top of their right hands and, as they slip their right hands away, take the right reins in their left hands. The reins should be short enough so that the horse can be stopped with a slight pull, but there should be no tension as long as he stands still. Usually, five-sixths of the class will understand how to hold the reins with the first explanation, but there is always at least one child who will not.

The next step is placing the bight of the reins and the crop, if the rider has one, to the left side of the horse's neck. This prevents the ends of the reins from dragging across the withers during the dismount.

Part of the mane should be held along with the reins in the left hand. The right hand rests in the hollow of the saddle above the right stirrup leather. Since her left

Throughout the dismount the rider keeps her right hand in the hollow of the saddle above the right stirrup leather, her left hand with the reins on the mane.

The rider should swing her leg high over her horse's back.

Each rider puts her weight on her hands as she takes her left foot out of the stirrup. Both feet should be together.

Dismounting and Mounting

hand is touching the horse, the rider feels any movement the horse intends to make, and can correct him.

Her hands help support her weight when she stands upright in her stirrups. Neither her knee nor her foot should touch the horse as she swings her right leg, stretched straight, above her horse's back.

Watch carefully for neatness and balance as your riders dismount. When their legs come together on the left side of their horses, each child should be standing easily on one stirrup. As she leans against her horse and rests her weight on her hands, each rider should still be upright, her elbows should be straight and her feet together.

Riders should slide to the ground with their sides against the saddles so that they are facing the front of their horses. No loud thumps should signal when the riders have hit the ground. Finally, everyone takes her horse at the bit, being careful not to lose hold of her horse's reins. The reins should be taken off the horses' necks if the children will be leading their horses or holding them for other riders.

A small child needs to lengthen her right rein before dismounting. This prevents her from jerking on the bit as her hand slides down the horse's neck while she is dropping to the ground during her dismount.

Mistakes in dismounting will catch your eye in almost every lesson. One child will shorten her reins so much before she dismounts that she makes her horse back. Another will lean across the saddle when she is trying to take her left foot out of the stirrup. Still another will bring her knee through the middle of the saddle or hold the pommel through the tree with her right hand.

Beginning riders sometimes kick the croups of their horses in their eagerness to dismount. These girls should straighten their knees and balance better with their weight on their hands so they are able to lift their legs high. If you hold a child's ankle and swing her leg back and forth

The rider slides to the ground with her side against the saddle so that she faces the front of her horse as she lands.

The rider should take her horse at the bit after her dismount.

Beginning riders sometimes kick the croups of their horses while dismounting.

above her horse's croup, she feels how to do it for herself.

A child who has trouble keeping her balance while taking her left foot from the stirrup needs individual instruction. Often the first time a rider dismounts, her trouble is caused by fear. Her hand wobbles on the horse's neck and the look on her face says, "I'm standing on nothing ten feet in the air." Stop her when she is halfway through her dismount. By resting your weight against her to hold her close to the horse, your hands are freed to show her how to stiffen her elbows so she can balance on her hands and take her foot from the stirrup at the same time.

Some children have been taught to move their hands onto the saddle halfway through the dismount. The movement is unnecessary. It also means the child must lengthen her reins and lose control while she is unbalanced.

An advanced rider can give you your worst headaches in dismounting. Her confidence suddenly makes her cocky. One day she will shock you by dropping her reins on her

Catch the child at the half-way point of the dismount if she has trouble keeping her balance in order to take her foot out of the stirrup.

Iceland ponies will tolerate a rider mounting on either side. (Ponies owned by Mrs. Judith Schmidt.)

Dismounting and Mounting

horse's neck and swinging her leg across her horse's withers, as she makes a flying leap for the ground. If the horse fails to make a flying leap in the air, you give thanks.

Even instructors and children who own their own horses do foolish things. I was told about Dora, who had been a riding assistant for a summer. She had her own horse that she trusted completely. With a leap and a bound she would land on his croup to dismount or mount, sliding off or clambering on. Her horse had become adjusted to odd happenings, but what if everyone in class imitated her?

Once a class is over, do not let your riders escape without helping either to put the horses in their stalls or to mount the next class. Even the child who says, "Please hold my horse for me. Mommy is waiting," should be kept in the ring. Riding is a time of sharing, of giving of yourself for someone else. Mommy wants this, too, even if she does have to wait for it.

Instructors tend to think of certain riding techniques as sacred. Does not everyone mount a horse on the left side? At an exhibition of Iceland ponies in Connecticut, the riders from Iceland mounted their horses on the right.

I asked one of the men, "Do you always mount on the right side?"

He looked surprised. "Oh, from either side," he said.

Coordination as well as balance are needed to mount a horse correctly. It is not strength that enables a rider to mount, but the way she times her upward jump with the pull of her arms.

Before they mount, children should check their girths. It may seem strange that it is necessary to remind them, but children should take the reins, too, before they mount, even if someone else is holding the horse. Again, the reins should be crossed through a child's left hand as they were for her dismount, and she should hold part of the mane.

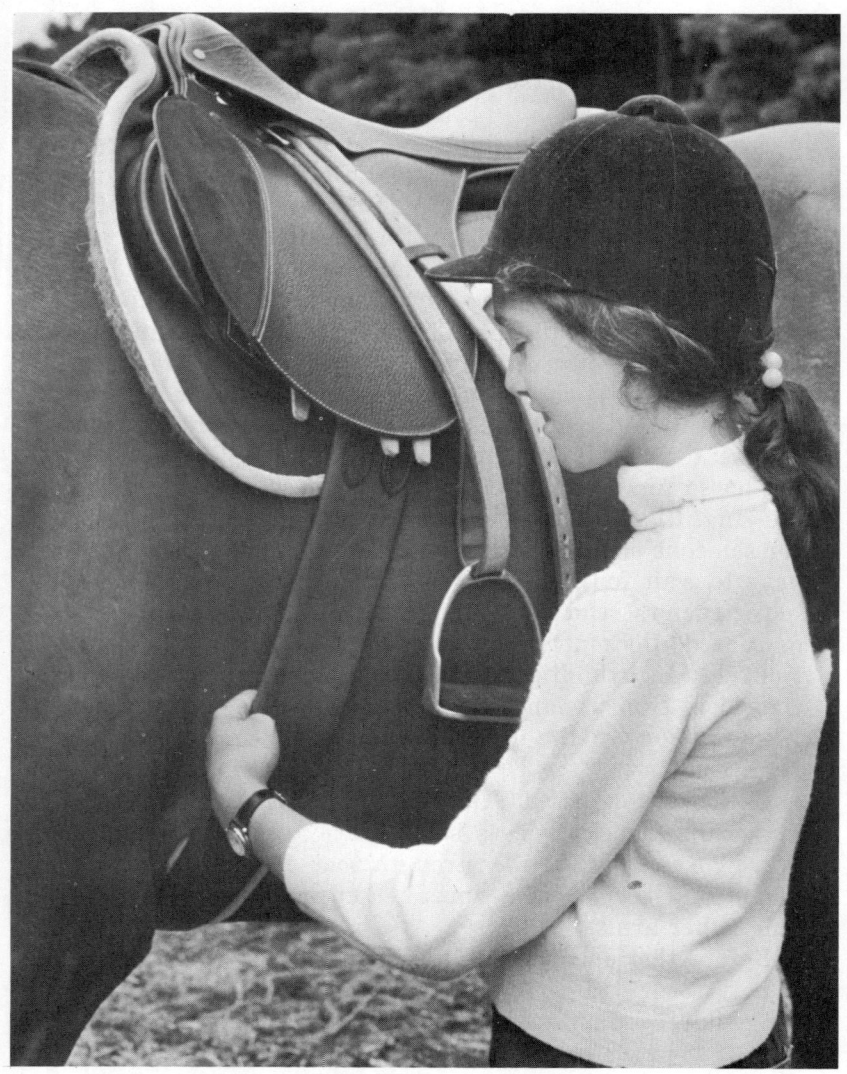

Before she mounts the rider checks her girth to see if she can put four fingers underneath it.

Dismounting and Mounting 91

Most children need to lengthen their stirrups a few holes in order to reach them. It is not necessary to run the buckle back into place until the stirrup is readjusted

The reins should be crossed through her left hand before she puts her hand on the mane.

She may need to lengthen her stirrup a few holes in order to put her foot in it.

after mounting. Often a child needs to hold her stirrup while she is putting her foot into it.

Facing the rear of her horse, the rider puts her right hand across the pommel, takes a hop and a jump as she pulls upward with both hands. Small children, who are

Dismounting and Mounting

often the quickest to learn how to mount with ease, may hold the stirrup leather if they are unable to reach the saddle.

The motion of mounting should be one continuous swing

She faces the rear of her horse and puts her right hand across the pommel of the saddle.

that includes lifting the right leg over the horse's back and sitting down gently in the saddle.

Most riders want to fix their stirrups as soon as they are mounted, but the reins are more important because they mean control. The reins should be untwisted, even, and the right length. The bight should be shifted to the right side of the horse's neck. Only then should the rider worry about the length of her stirrups.

Children become quite ingenious when allowed to do something by themselves. When my daughter was about as high as the belly of the horse she liked to ride, she devised her own system for mounting. I can still picture her standing beside the biggest horse her grandparents owned, her blond ponytail in contrast to the horse's black coat. She would take the reins, long reins it is true, but

Mounting should be one continuous-motion swing that includes lifting the right leg over the horse's back and sitting down gently in the saddle.

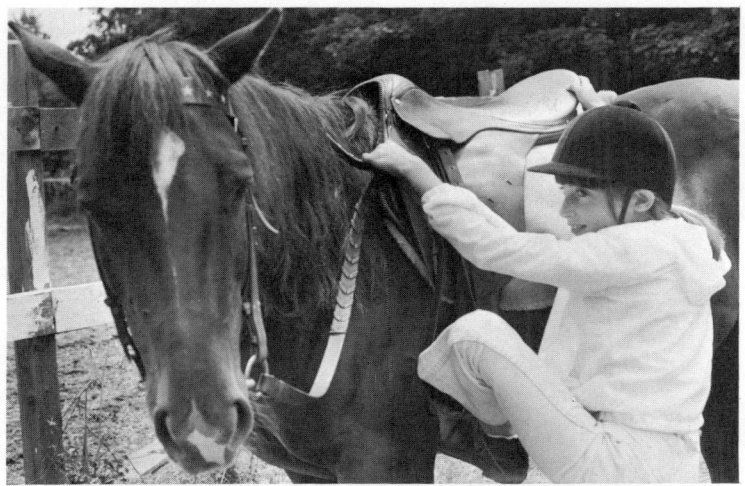

A careless child may kick her horse in the side with her toe if she faces the front of her horse and has her hand on the back of the saddle.

let him take a step and she showed him she meant him to stand still! She would catch the stirrup leather in both hands, give a mighty jump and tuck her knee in the stirrup. From there she could just reach the mane and the top of the saddle. It was a big upward haul, but she would do it alone, completing her mounting in about four seconds.

Some of the important points you will need to correct when a class mounts are kicking a horse on the croup, jamming a toe in his side, facing the front of the horse tempting him to cow kick, forgetting to hold the reins, and grabbing the saddle by the tree. Sometimes a child will twist her stirrup leather the wrong way, but she usually discovers it is twisted as soon as she has mounted. If you pretend not to notice that her stirrup is too long for her to get her leg across the horse's back, she will probably step down again and put the stirrup up a couple of holes for herself.

Your riders should know how to shorten the rein on the off side to prevent a horse from nipping while a rider is mounting.

Dismounting and Mounting

Sometimes, of course, the horse causes trouble. If a horse starts to back up when a child is trying to mount, make sure her reins are not too tight so that she is asking him to back. If the horse is to blame, show her how to stand him in a corner with his rump against the fence so he cannot back up. Usually, he will be cured when his stalling tactics fail.

A horse sometimes moves around in circles. The child may have one rein so short the horse thinks she wants him to turn. However, if the horse is trying to prevent a rider from mounting by moving around, the child needs to give a firm tug on the reins to stop him, then mount quickly before he takes another step. Sometimes a rider needs to mount in spite of the horse's movement; then check him firmly as soon as she is in the saddle. If he is unable to prevent his rider from mounting and is corrected immediately, he soon learns he is wasting his effort and being punished besides. A horse should be made to stand still after his rider mounts. A horse that races off the instant there is weight on the saddle is unsafe.

Though your horses may not try to nip riders while they are mounting, your riders should know how to shorten the rein on the off side so that a horse cannot reach them to take a bite of their arms.

The reluctant rider who only mounts a horse if he is sleeping on his feet needs to discover what she already knows. Let her have a horse who moves a little, or will turn around if not checked, then turn your attention to the rest of the class and leave her alone. She will not like to be the only girl who cannot mount by herself. Usually, her determination not to be outdone will get her mounted. How proud she feels then! Do remember to praise her.

One wise horsewoman, who had been teaching children to ride for over 40 years, used to stress the importance of mounting correctly. She owned a hunter named Jack, a lanky horse that was famed for jumping over cars

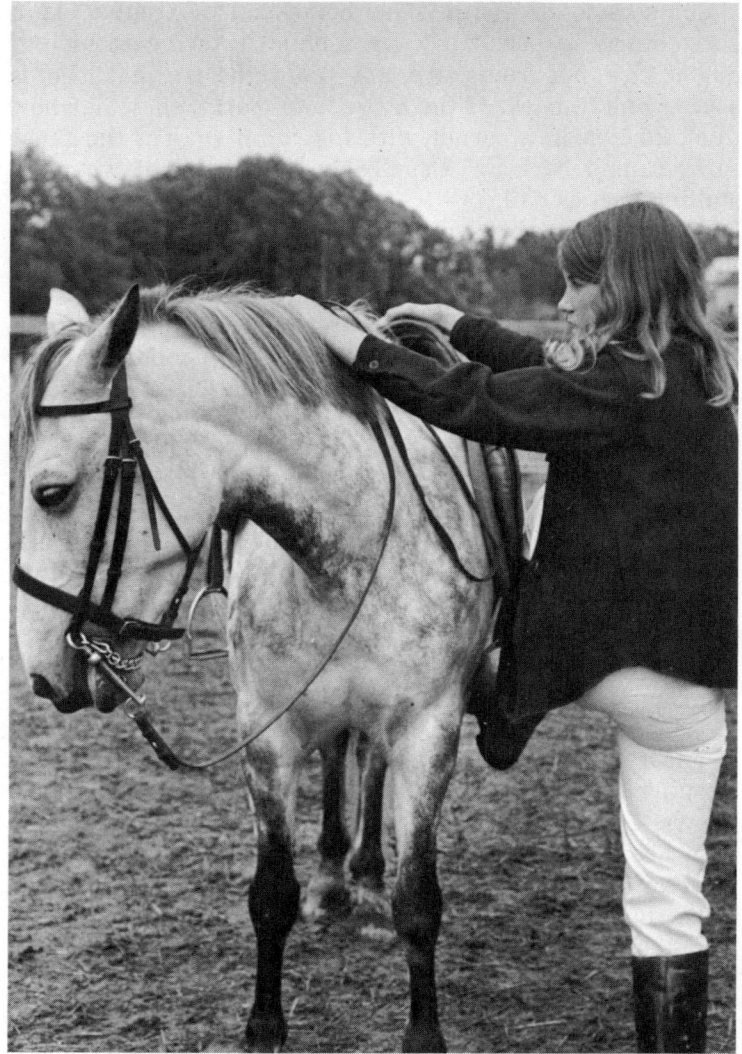

Be careful the rider does not grab the tree of the saddle to help her mount.

Dismounting and Mounting

The game of "Pig," which gives practice in dismounting is a favorite game with children.

parked in the driveway. On jumping days he was the most popular horse in the stable.

She would choose a cocky rider among those who begged to ride Jack. "Now," she would tell the group, "if you see this girl make a mistake in mounting, you may ride Jack instead of her."

What thought that girl put into mounting! How carefully everyone watched her! When she had finished, the horsewoman would say, "Didn't anyone see a mistake? She made three."

After the mistakes were pointed out, the other children would groan, "Why didn't we see that?"

One of the games you can play that gives a class practice with dismounting and mounting is called "Pig." It is a silent game with winning dependent on how carefully a child watches you. Every motion of the horse has a signal given by the instructor. A back and forth motion with the hands as if playing the piano and crossing over and back with both hands means walk. An up and down motion, as if playing cymbals, means trot. With advanced riders, a circular motion with one hand around the other means canter. A large circle, using your whole arm, means reverse. A large circle with both arms means circle. Holding up one hand as a policeman does means stop. Both thumbs pointed down is the signal for dismount. One thumb pointed down into the palm of one hand is dismount halfway. Both thumbs raised says mount, a signal always accompanied by sighs of relief from the riders. Each time a child fails to obey a signal, or fails to make her horse obey, she acquires a letter, first a "P," then an "I," and finally a "G." When she has three letters, she must walk her horse until the game is over. The winner is the last rider left in the game.

There is one other way to mount: get a leg up. A leg up is a simple method for hoisting a rider onto a horse. Your riders sometimes need a leg up because it is quick

A rider must keep her upper leg straight when a helper lifts her by the knee and ankle in order to give her a leg up.

The rider who bends her upper leg is hard to lift for a leg up.

Dismounting and Mounting

if you are in a rush to start a class; or if they are riding bareback; or if one of them has a sore foot and cannot step hard on the stirrup; or a dozen other reasons.

A child who is being given a leg up stands beside the horse, ready to catch the saddle as soon as she is lifted. She bends her left knee, but keeps the upper part of her leg stiff and straight. The instructor holds her leg with one hand under her knee, the other around her ankle. On the count of three, the child jumps as high as she can and the instructor lifts her upward by her leg.

A child who bends her upper leg or does not jump is heavy to lift. Set her down again, even if you could lift her easily, so that she learns how to cooperate when given a leg up.

A woman who had been a trick rider for many years was once asked for a leg up by a heavy lady. The trick rider gave her such a boost that the lady went right across the horse's back to land on her feet on his other side.

I asked the trick rider, "What did you do then?"

She laughed. "Gave the lady a leg up from the other side."

Whenever you are giving lessons in mounting and dismounting, stress the importance of quiet movements around horses. The way a child mounts indicates the way she will ride. If her hands are quiet and assured as she takes the reins and if she swings on smoothly and sits down without a thump, the horse feels reassured that he will be kindly treated during the ride. If both horse and rider get off to a good start, the entire lesson will be a happy one.

6

CONTROL THROUGH FIGURES AND GAMES

The intermediate ring is the place in which a beginning rider, who has learned how to post, is taught to make her horse obey.

A riding assistant once said, "Oh, don't put me in the intermediate ring to teach. These girls already know how to trot and you won't let me teach them to canter. What else is there?"

The riding director shook her head. "There are circles and turns, correct diagonals at a trot, and most important of all, learning how to make a horse obey," she said. "It can be fun, too. Children enjoy such simple things, relays and games, drill teams and riding in pairs."

Whatever you teach to intermediates has, as its aim, control of the horse. A rider needs to know how to make a stubborn horse go, how to keep a horse close to the fence when he wants to use the middle of the ring, how to trot although the rest of the class is standing still.

A great advantage of group riding is the opportunity it offers students to ride different types of horses. I have watched children learn control in an intermediate ring with a group of horses which varied the problems the riders faced each day. There was White Magic, a lazy horse who refused to move unless his rider was willing to kick in a way he could feel. Pherion was just the opposite. He would trot at the lightest leg pressure. Woe betide the rider who kicked him. Keeta was a "push-but-

Control Through Figures and Games

ton" horse, who knew better than the rider what she should do. The cleverest horse in the group was Eager Ears, who put no more effort into the ride than his rider demanded. Ears, as he was nicknamed, would jump five feet as easily as a child jumps into a mound of hay, or he would refuse to trot more than three steps at a time if his rider thought he was stupid.

An intermediate rider finds a challenge in learning to turn her horse correctly or in trying to win a game. She understands the objective and while she is seeking it, she learns to control her horse. Her first experience in working her horse independently makes her realize it is up to her to make her horse go *when* she asks and *where* she wants him to go.

One of the first lessons intermediates should be taught is how to make a horse trot. First, the rider should shorten the reins. When a horse trots, he tucks his head more than he does at a walk, so that the rider needs shorter reins to have the same control at a trot as she had at a walk. A horse always feels his rider shorten the reins and this movement alone signals him that something is about to happen. He perks up and pays attention.

When the rider asks for the trot, she releases the reins slightly to be sure she has no pressure on them. She shifts her weight forward and uses leg pressure by squeezing the calves of her legs against the horse's sides.

Horses, however, are smart enough to know when their riders are too weak or unwilling to force them to work. Often a child must resort to punishment—a kick—to convince her horse she means business. When she kicks, she is not shooing flies with a gentle swish, but saying, "Move, horse." The edge of her heel should dig into his side behind the girth with a hard, sharp kick. She may need to give him a half-dozen staccato kicks to convince him she is determined he obey. Sometimes she may even need a crop or green stick on his shoulder.

Intermediate riders should not be taught to use a crop

The edge of the rider's heel should dig into her horse's side behind the girth with a hard, sharp kick.

Control Through Figures and Games

behind the saddle because this backward movement upsets their balance entirely. They concentrate so hard on where they are hitting their horses, they forget to use their legs, their heels fly high, their reins flap. Furthermore, some horses buck when hit on the rear. Intermediate riders are not yet able to cope with bucking horses.

Once a horse discovers his rider is able to make him trot, he usually is willing to trot without being kicked. A rider must remember to use leg pressure first every time she wants her horse to move, even if she had to kick him the previous time she trotted. Making a horse go for leg pressure alone is a basic lesson of control.

Sometimes a horse will trot for a few steps, then walk again, and nothing the rider does will make him do more than a fast walk. This same horse will be the one that cuts corners or trots around the middle of the ring instead of staying close to the fence. His rider needs to learn that before she can make her horse trot, she has to make him go where she tells him to go. This means she makes up her mind where she is going to trot and uses her reins to force her horse there. She may need to shorten one rein until her hand is a dozen inches from the bit. She may need to turn her horse around and walk him straight to the fence, not at an angle that lets him almost get away with his will. Sometimes a child has to ride with her outside rein shorter than her inside rein in order to keep her horse from cutting corners. Of all the qualities a rider needs when she is on a willful horse, determination is the most important. As soon as she can force her horse to walk beside the fence and into the corners, she can also make him trot.

It is as important to know how to stop a horse correctly as how to make him move. A rider's weight must be used to stop a horse. Since a person's head is the heaviest part of her body, if a rider puts back her head, her weight is shifted backward. Even before she pulls on the reins to stop her horse, a child should shift her weight backward.

After she shifts her weight, she should shorten the reins and then pull toward herself, her hands low, her pull steady. As soon as the horse stops, she should release the pressure on the reins.

An instructor who visited the Greenwich Pony Club taught the riders to lean halfway back to their horses' tails, then sit up again. The riders were able to feel, as they sat up slowly, how much they had shifted their weight. Within 10 minutes of practice, all of the horses were stopping without the riders touching their reins. One girl told her mother that after that day her horse stopped for her, even from a canter, as soon as she put her weight back.

Another instructor taught her students to lift their chins when stopping their horses. This put their weight back. A woman came to her for a private lesson in how to stop a runaway horse. During the lesson the woman was taught to put her head back. She was asked to walk 10 steps, shift her weight, stop her horse, then walk again. For an hour she walked 10 steps, stopped, walked again.

When she paid for the lesson, the woman said, "But my horse runs away at a gallop, not at a walk."

"Go home and practice stopping at a walk just as you did here," the instructor said.

A week later the woman returned, pride in her smile. "It worked," she said. "My horse never runs away now."

A child uses her weight to back a horse just as she does to stop him. Leg pressure is used in front of the girth. A child's eyes should be up and she should look ahead of her. Her pull should be equal on both reins. Sometimes a horse needs guidance to back straight. Leg pressure behind the girth on one side will move him away from that leg, just as a shove with one hand will move him over in his stall.

A child who is not using her weight to stop or back

The rider keeps her weight back, her eyes up, when she pulls on the reins to back her horse.

her horse is usually looking down to watch her hands. Sometimes a child urges her horse forward with her weight forward, while at the same time she pulls on the reins to stop him. If a child's hands go up in the air while she is stopping her horse, her elbows will go out, and you will notice her reins are too long. One of the most common mistakes a child makes is to ask a horse to stop by pulling on the reins, when she really wants him to go and is kicking him.

After a child knows the correct way to start and stop her horse, she should learn how to use her weight when she turns. She should turn her head to look where she is going. By turning her head she shifts her weight; she also sees where she is taking the horse. She should shorten the inside rein, the one toward the turn. When she pulls, her hand should be close to her horse. The rider uses her inside leg to press the horse's hindquarters away from the turn, so that he follows with his whole body.

There are many figures and games that develop the

A common mistake is to lean forward when pulling on the reins to stop a horse.

Control Through Figures and Games   111

basic skills of control. The first figure is to turn with all the horses in the line also turning. Next, the rider learns to turn her horse around and walk him in the other direction. Finally, she learns to turn him at a trot.

The circle is the second figure to teach. While the class is lined up at one end of the ring, let each child, in turn, walk and then trot her horse in a circle. The riders should work on circles until they are able to make round ones without hesitation in the horses' gaits. The entire class should then be asked to circle at a walk and a trot. This presents new problems. The horses need more room to circle at a trot than at a walk, and each child must be far enough away from the other horses to avoid a collision.

Next, the riders should learn to reverse toward the fence. This is one figure that is taught most easily by demonstration. Have one child walk her horse beside the

Sometimes a rider, trying to make her horse walk, mistakenly pulls on the reins and kicks the horse at the same time.

The rider should look in the same direction she is turning her horse.

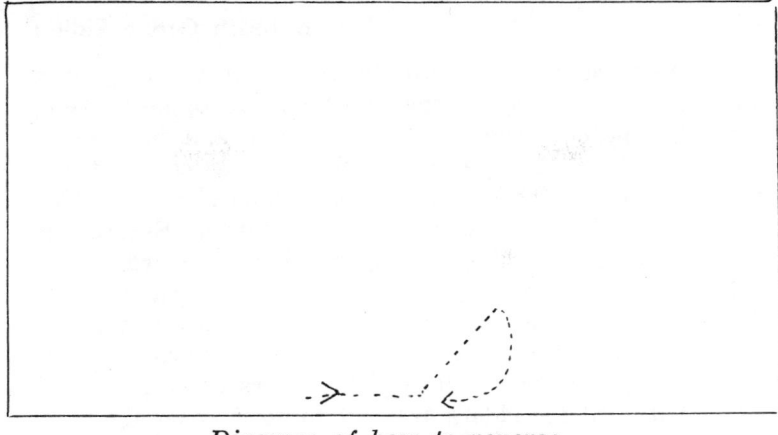

Diagram of how to reverse.

A rider may reverse in a ring: (1) by walking her horse left from the fence at a 45-degree angle; (2) by turning right toward the fence again; (3) going right along the fence in the opposite direction.

fence. She should turn into the center of the ring at a 45 degree angle. Next, she shortens the opposite rein, turns her head in the opposite direction, and returns toward the fence. Before she reaches the fence she turns to walk back in the direction from which she came. The simile of a clock sometimes helps children. Before the reverse, a child will be walking her horse toward 12:00. When he begins to reverse, he heads between 10 and 11:00. As soon as there is enough room, she walks him past 11 until he is facing 3:00. Finally, as she approaches the fence, she turns toward 6:00. The reverse, too, should be practiced until the riders are able to do it smoothly at an even gait at a trot. Few accomplishments give you a

A rider should post on the outside diagonal. She rises from her saddle when the foreleg toward the fence is forward. (1) the last horse: his inside foreleg is forward, rider is in the saddle; (2) Second horse: outside foreleg is forward, the rider is out of saddle at height of her posting. (3) first horse. Outside foreleg is starting forward, rider is starting to rise from saddle.

Control Through Figures and Games

greater sense of triumph than seeing 10 or 15 horses trot reverses without conflict and without stopping.

Your riders now have enough control of their horses to add a new technique. They should learn diagonals. By this time, most children know that a horse trots with diagonal legs, his right front leg moving with his left rear leg. A judge in a horse show checks a rider to see if she knows diagonals, because a rider must have balance when she changes direction as well as control. In a horse show class, a rider should post on the outside diagonal. When the outside front leg of her horse, the front leg toward the fence, is reaching forward, the child should be out of the saddle at the highest position of her posting. Every change in direction means a change in the diagonal on which she posts.

Teach diagonals by having a child watch her horse's shoulder. As the outside shoulder moves forward, she should be rising from the stirrups. Usually, a child finds it easier to stand up in a trotting position until that shoulder is forward and to sit down as the shoulder moves back. Sometimes a child only discovers how to post to the outside diagonal by sitting down and bouncing for several beats, then standing as his shoulder moves forward and his beat lifts her out of the saddle.

When a child does start to post, tell her if she is on the correct diagonal. Let her watch the outside shoulder until she recognizes how it moves forward as she is standing up. Have her take her trotting position for a few strides, then post once more. See if she is able to tell on which diagonal she is posting.

A young girl who was teaching diagonals discovered one child in her class who could not tell when the horse's shoulder was forward and when it was back. In desperation the instructor said, "Well, then, lean way forward and tell me when your horse's foot hits the ground." The child told her at each step. "All right, now post and be

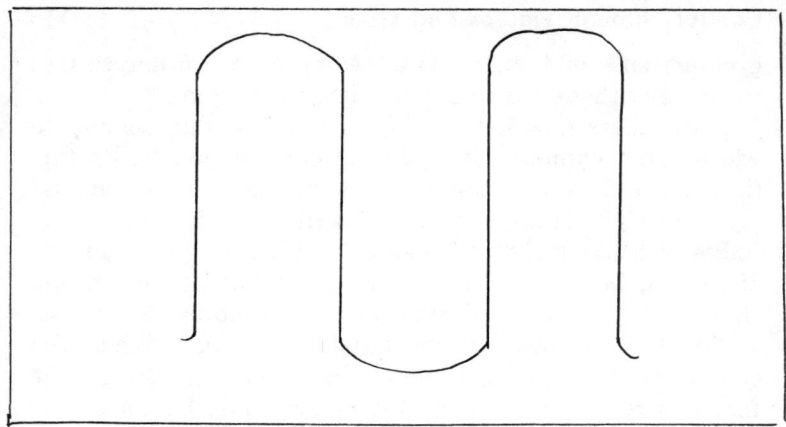

Diagram: A line of horses trotting serpentines weave in half circles which have parallel sides.

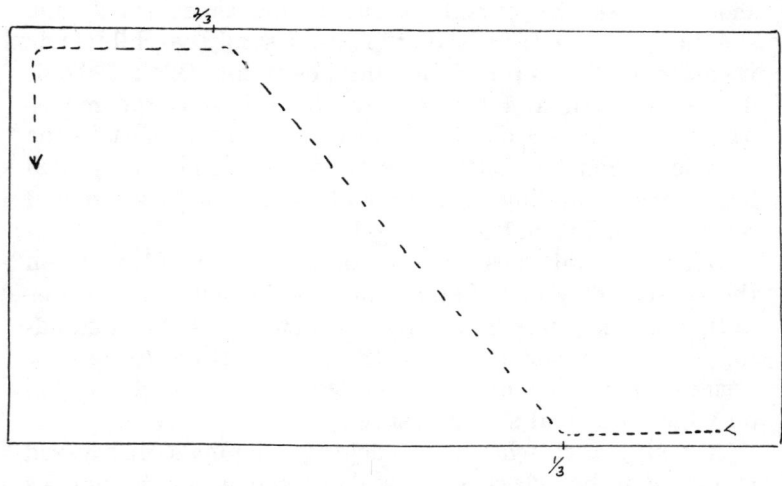

Diagram: A line of horses begins a change of direction 1/3 of the way down one side of the ring, crosses the ring diagonally to a spot 2/3 of the way from the end of the ring, which results in the horses' going in the other direction.

Control Through Figures and Games 117

sure you hit the saddle when his outside hoof hits the ground." The child learned diagonals.

Illogical as it seems, occasionally a child is unable to tell diagonals with the outside shoulder, but is able to tell them with the inside shoulder because she is permitted to sit down as the shoulder goes forward.

To change diagonals, a child should either stand for a beat or sit a double bounce in the saddle. Once your riders know how to tell diagonals and how to change them, be sure they change whenever the horses change direction.

As you teach figures which help a child's control, she will also be gaining practice on diagonals. As riding becomes more complex, your riders are learning that they need to remember many things at once. One of the simpler figures that combines control with drill on diagonals is serpentines. Serpentines are actually a series of half-circles in which a line of horses weaves in and out with the motion of a snake. The sides of each loop should be parallel to each other. Before each turn, the riders change diagonals.

A "change of direction" using the entire ring is as much a game as "follow-the-leader" if you choose different girls to lead the group and call for a change at unexpected moments. The horse leading the group begins to cut diagonally across the ring when he is one-third of the way down one side. He reaches the far side of the ring at a point two-thirds of the way down the ring. Although he continues to move in the same direction, when he comes around the corner, the line will have reversed. The riders will change diagonals while crossing the ring. You can have two lines working at once, which is more fun for the riders.

Drill teams are also challenging. Begin by having the children ride in pairs. Next, as if you were having a grand march, let them come down the center of the ring by fours. At the far end of the ring, they split into twos. The next time down the center have one couple from the

The Virginia reel can be adapted to the riding ring. First step: the horses come forward and the riders bow to their partners.

Musical chairs is a good game for rainy days. Children with outstretched arms to be touched may be used for "chairs."

Control Through Figures and Games

left go first, then a couple from the right follow. At the far end, let them divide into single file. Each child should watch her partner as she goes around the ring, keeping her horse opposite her all the way, until they join in the middle again. As the children's control improves, have them trot part of the time and use more complex formations.

The Virginia Reel can also be adapted to a riding ring. The partners come forward to bow, then back their horses into place again. Each girl rides around her partner, holding her right hand on one turn, her left on the next. The head couple trots down the center of the two lines and back, then each one leads her line around to the opposite end. There the other girls pass two by two between the horses of the head couple.

Some of the simple games of children become exciting when played with horses. The game "Come Over" uses one child as "it." The girl who is "it" should use colors and tack from the horses when she calls for girls to come over while she tries to catch them. For example, she may say, "Let all those with black manes come over" or "Let all those with double bridles come over." The girl who is "it" only needs to tag a horse or child to make her help catch the others. As soon as the class is secure at a walk, "Come Over" can be played at a trot.

Walking races, trotting races without stirrups, races that involve mounting at one end and dismounting at the other end of the ring, races that give practice in the emergency dismount at a walk, all improve the riders' skills.

One of the most popular activities for intermediates is mock jumping. Two burlap bags are used for jump standards, a thin stick for the bar. A second set of bags a few yards away makes a mock in and out jump. The riders must take trotting positions over the jumps.

Many of these games can be played at a walk on rainy

Snatch the Bacon can be played with two teams. A rider from one team carries "the bacon"—a shirt or burlap bag—while the rider from the other team tries to snatch it from her.

days. Most of them can be adapted for advanced riders as well as for intermediates. "Musical chairs" is good for rainy days. Either children with outstretched arms to be touched, or burlap bags on the ground on which a child must stand after she dismounts, are used for "chairs."

When my son was teaching intermediate riders, he used to invent new games every time it rained. As a result, few instructors were more popular than he. The game the children enjoyed most was "Snatch the Bacon." The bacon was a burlap bag or a rag or a handkerchief in his hand. He would call two girls to compete. The one who could reach the bacon first and get it out of his hand won. The horses were often leery of the rag, so that the children had to reassure them, urge them forward, and use every device they had learned to outsmart a horse. Of course,

Control Through Figures and Games

to the other riders, the horses' behavior was the funniest part of the game.

"Snatch the bacon" could also be played with two teams. One side was given the bacon. If a child on the opposite team snatched the bacon for herself, the point went to her team.

The intermediate ring is a fun ring for instructors and children. No two days are ever alike. The most valuable lesson the riders will ever learn—how to control horses—is the one you are teaching. You will come to know your riders through the laughter which comes from playing games and outsmarting a horse when the rider's skill and will are stronger than his.

7

THE RIDER PREPARES FOR A LESSON

Though your primary concern may be teaching riding, if you have large groups of riders, the riders themselves must help prepare the horses for a lesson. They should help take horses to and from the rings, check tack, and adjust stirrups. Some class time must be given to these details until the riders are so schooled in the safety measures involved that you no longer feel the entire responsibility.

Courtesy is safety where horses are concerned. More experienced riders should help the beginners in handling their horses in the stable area. One riding camp includes a certain number of points for helpfulness and cooperation in the tests that children must pass in order to advance to another ring. Riders who are about to leave the ring should give a leg up, or hold a horse or a gate when needed. If a child is having trouble with her horse, whether she is leading him, or mounting him, or taking him through the gate, other riders should keep their horses out of her way.

Horses should always be kept the proper distance from one another in the stable area and especially around the drinking trough. While horses are being led, a child is more accessible to the heels of a kicking horse than when she is mounted. The horse may be aiming at another horse, but a child can get in the way.

"May I help?" is a welcome question to any instructor. The small voice from the child who wants to help should

The Rider Prepares for a Lesson

not be ignored no matter how busy you are. If you take a moment to show her how to help, you will never regret it. The child may be standing in front of her house, tugging on both reins while she stares him in the eyes. She tells you, "I'm going to give Jacques a drink of water." Show her how to lead him without looking in his eyes by walking on his left side, her right hand at the bit, her left hand holding the loose reins so he will not step on them. If her horse is stubborn, show her how to lead him from side to side, using her weight against his shoulder, until he takes a step.

An overly eager horse can be kept from barging into his stablemates or stepping on the toes of the child who leads him if the child will keep her elbow against his shoulder as she walks. If the horse is anxious to reach the watering trough, she can walk him in circles until it is his turn.

My daughter's first horse was a big black Morgan,

A rider's horse will not walk if she looks him in the eye.

She should lead her horse with her right hand at the bit and the loose ends of the reins in her left hand so the horse will not step on them.

A stubborn horse may need to be led from side to side until he takes a step.

Chewbit, who had so little concern about where he walked my husband called him "Sherman Tank." If he stepped on someone's shoe, Chewbit discovered, the shoe was quickly removed, so why should he worry about it? Chewbit is still stepping on toes in his unconcerned manner, then giving the girl he has hurt a loving look with his big black eyes. When a little child is about to lead a Chewbit-type horse, send along a more experienced rider to help her put him in his stall.

When the children lead their horses into the ring, have them use the center of the ring for mounting. By using the center the riders leave room for those who are mounted to ride by the fence. There is also plenty of room to keep the horses away from each other. The horses, too, are trained. They associate the center of the ring, rather than the fence, with the place to stop.

The necessity for avoiding the fence as a refuge was driven home to me by Tahana, a fine-boned thoroughbred. Tahana held a special place in my heart because I had been given the colt she had foaled in a snowstorm as a wedding present. Months later, a little girl climbed on Tahana without permission. When Tahana was startled, the child screamed. The horse raced for the fence. Driven by the child's continued screams, Tahana jumped. As she came over the top of the fence, her foreleg hit. The child was rolled to the ground, unhurt, but Tahana broke her leg.

Not only should your riders avoid mounting near the fence, they should never mount outside the ring. A mixture of mounted and unmounted riders is always dangerous and difficult to supervise in the stable area.

The riders need to check their tack as part of the routine of class work. The keepers on the bridle should be fastened. The curb chain should be untwisted. When it is smooth, it should be fastened so there is slack in it.

The saddle pad should be under the front of the saddle where it protects the horse's withers. If it has slipped out

All the keepers on the bridle should be fastened.

A twisted curb chain should be untwisted . . .

until it lies flat.

of place, the child should resaddle the horse. If the saddle itself has slipped off the withers, she should resaddle, also. Children often groan at the time wasted in resaddling, but if the rule is enforced, they quickly become proficient.

The girth should be tightened equally on both sides of the saddle. A child *does not tighten the girth only on the left side.* She must tighten it a hole or two on the right, then go around the horse to tighten it a hole on two on the left. She continues to tighten first one side, then the other, until the girth is tight. Explain to her that if she were to tighten the girth on one side only, the girth would pull the horse's skin to that side. This is uncomfortable for the horse. When she finishes tightening the girth, she should count the number of holes it has been raised to be sure the number is equal, or nearly equal, on both sides. She should be able to get four fingers under the girth when it is tight.

Next, she should stretch her horse's forelegs. She stands by his shoulder, puts her weight against him, and tugs above his knee with both hands until she has pulled his leg as high as she can lift it. This pulls the skin away from the girth and helps to prevent girth sores. The horses quickly accept this routine. One horse, Toreador, lifts his forelegs for his rider to stretch them just as a dog raises a paw to shake hands. Sassy, a saddlebred, will often stretch the second foreleg for herself after the rider finishes stretching the first one.

As soon as the rider has checked her horse's tack, she stands beside him to wait until you check, too. It only takes a minute to be sure she has done everything correctly. If she has missed one point, you move on to the next rider while she corrects her omission. Because this puts her at the end of the line again, your riders quickly learn to use care in preparing their horses for mounting.

In the intermediate ring the riders should adjust their own stirrups. Many a child will learn to measure the

The girth should be tightened equally on both sides.

The rider should count the number of holes the girth is tightened on both sides to make sure the number is the same (or different by only one hole).

The Rider Prepares for a Lesson

length of her stirrups before mounting by putting a thumb or finger at the top of the stirrup leather and touching the stirrup under her armpit. Her arm is usually the same length as her stirrup leather should be for her leg. She should not measure with a finger at the top of the saddle because this distance varies from saddle to saddle.

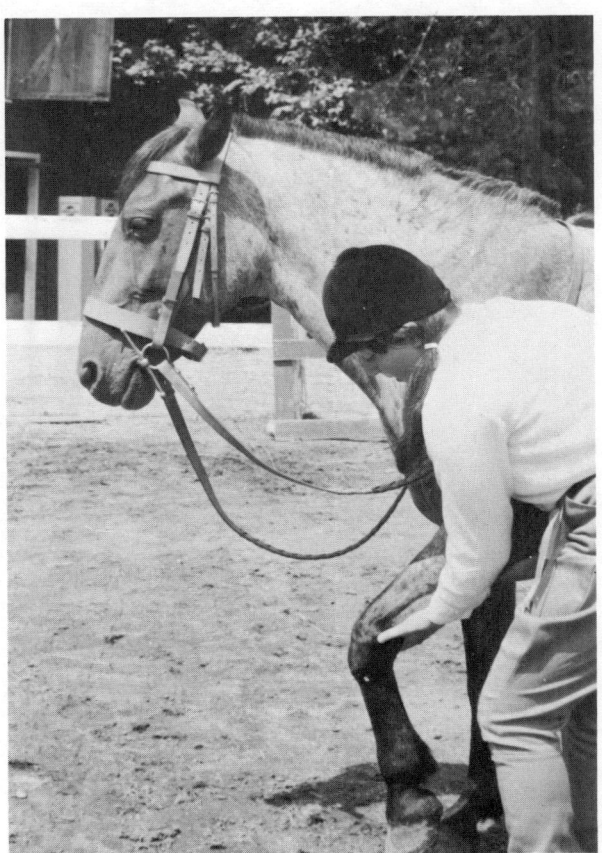

A rider should stretch her horse's forelegs by lifting each leg up and forward to stretch his skin away from the girth.

She measures the length of her stirrups from the top of the stirrup leather to her armpit.

The Rider Prepares for a Lesson

Most of the children will need to learn to adjust their stirrups after they have mounted. They will want to drop the reins and use both hands to fix the stirrups. "My horse won't go anywhere," one child in every class will say. But what would she do if he did?

The first step in adjusting stirrups from the saddle is to pull down the buckle to a place where the rider can unfasten it easily. Pressure with her foot will then lengthen her stirrup; a pull with her hand will shorten it. The first few times she tries to refasten the buckle in the proper hole, her fingers will fumble around a bit. Soon she will be able to do it without even watching her hand. Last, she lifts the stirrup leather below the buckle in order to have some slack in it, then pulls the buckle into place again by shoving her foot hard against the stirrup.

Small girls often discover stirrup leathers do not have holes high enough to make their stirrups short enough. Do not let these girls put their feet in the stirrup leathers, because their feet will not slip out of the leathers if the horse stumbles or they slide off. Punch a new hole. If the leather punch has vanished momentarily in someone's pocket or if the saddle belongs to someone who does not want new holes in the leathers, wrap the leathers. Unbuckle the stirrup leather, then wrap the end around the top of the stirrup. When you fasten the buckle again, be sure you wrapped the leather in such a way that the buckle is close to the saddle where it belongs.

The end of the stirrup leather should either be tucked in a keeper, or tucked behind the stirrup leather and pulled up high back of the rider's leg where it is out of the way.

The stirrup leather should lie flat against the rider's leg or boot. If it is twisted, her foot will be backward in the stirrup and the leather will cut against her leg. You can teach a class how to find the correct side of the stirrup if you first have everyone drop her stirrups. When

She lengthens her stirrup by pressure with her foot, or shortens it by pulling on the strap with her hand. She only needs one hand to adjust her stirrups.

She lifts the stirrup leather below the buckle in order to have some slack in it; a shove with her foot will pull the buckle into place close to the saddle.

Never put a child's foot in the leathers. Wrap the leather around the stirrup if you cannot punch a new hole.

If the keeper for the end of the stirrup leather is broken or the saddle does not have one, the end of the leather can be tucked behind the buckle . . .

and pulled tight back of the rider's leg.

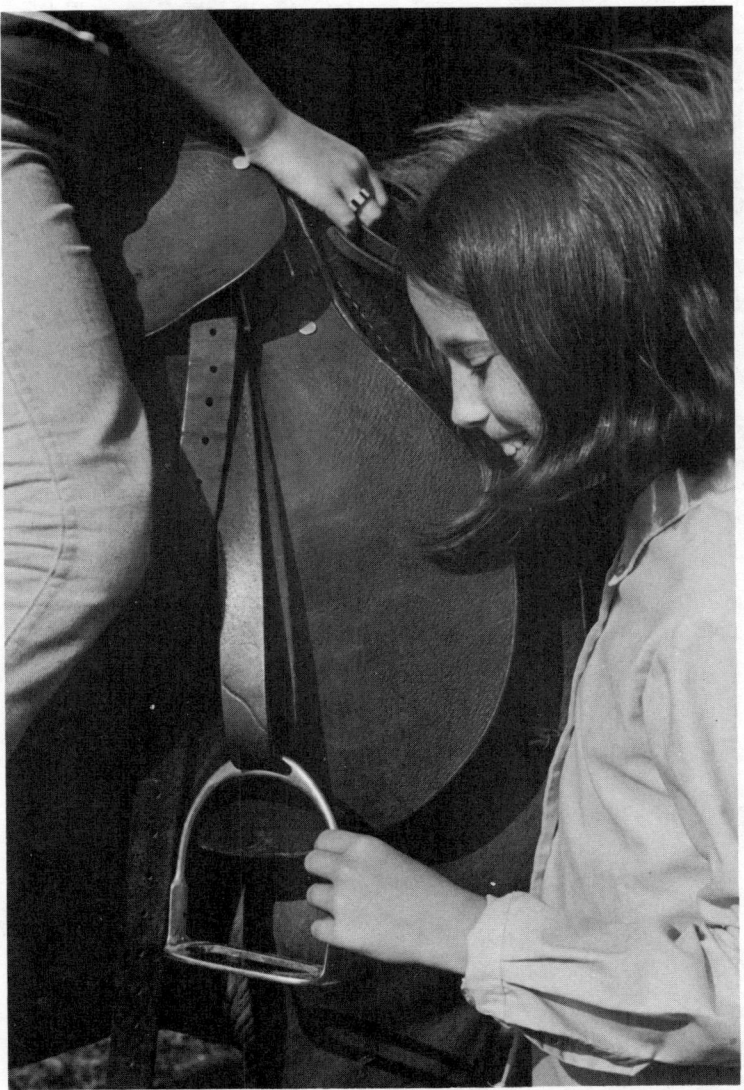

The side of the stirrup toward the horse's shoulder turns out.

The rider should check her girth once more by leaning down to put four fingers under it.

The Rider Prepares for a Lesson

If the girth is loose, the rider thrusts her leg forward, lifts the flap and pulls up on the billets.

the stirrup is lying parallel to the horse's side, a rider turns out the side toward the horse's shoulder, the "front" side, then puts her foot in the stirrup.

Before taking her horse to the fence to begin the lesson, the rider should check her girth once more. She should check it once in a while while she is riding, too.

While the class is walking at the beginning of the lesson, you will have a chance to explain to any new riders how to hold double reins. Usually, you introduce double reins in the intermediate ring.

A rider first straightens her reins, making sure there is no twist in them between the bit and her hands. She takes both of the reins as if they were one. Show her how a pull on the curb rein tightens the curb chain under the horse's chin. A pull on the snaffle, however, does not

(1) The first time you show a rider how to hold double reins have her take both of them as she would take single reins.

The Rider Prepares for a Lesson

(2) The reins should be untwisted; the snaffle (the top rein on the bit) is held outside the curb rein as the two lie beside the horse's neck.

tighten the chain. The snaffle rein goes outside the curb rein when the two reins come along the horse's neck into her hand. Whichever rein is on the outside receives the pull from her hand and, since she is not expecting to have difficulty controlling her horse, she wants the rein that pulls the easiest on the bit to be on the outside. To make sure she does not pull on the curb rein by mistake she should ride with the curb rein a little longer than the snaffle rein. The last step in holding double reins is to slip a baby finger between them.

Sometimes a horse will teach the rider to remember the hard pull of a curb rein. Eager Ears was a horse with a sensitive mouth and resented any misuse of the curb. One summer a child had trouble making Eager Ears go. He kept backing up. The rider became so angry that she

(3) After she makes sure her curb is looser than her snaffle, her baby finger goes between the two reins.

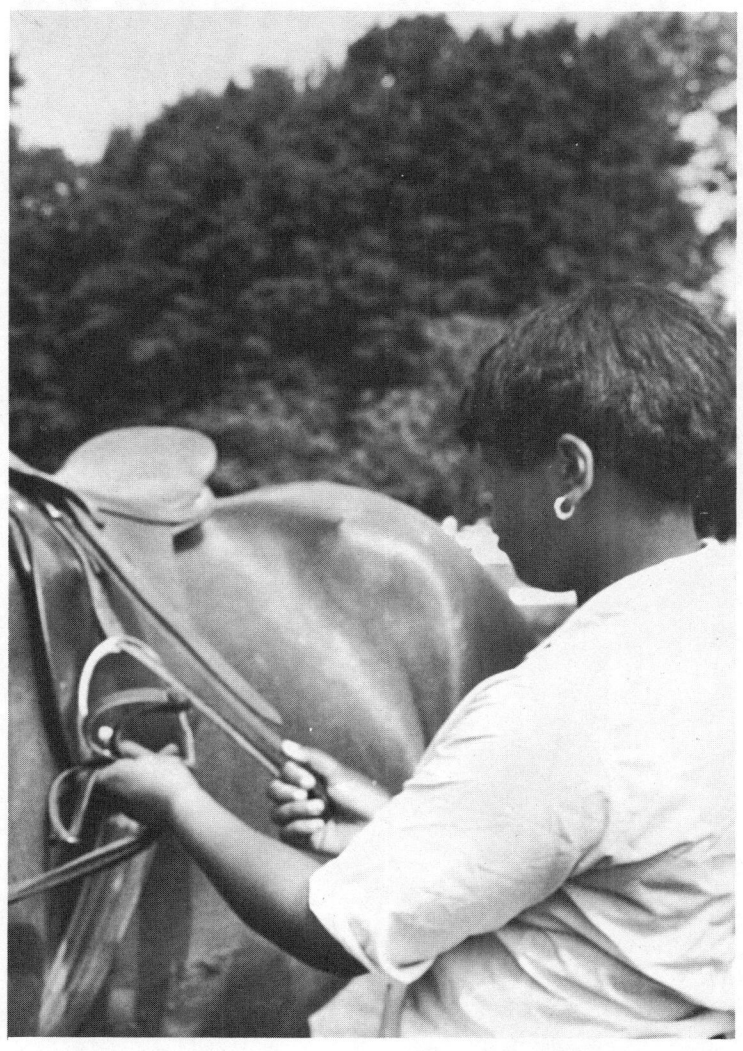

At the end of the lesson the rider runs the stirrups up the back of the leathers . . .

and tucks the leathers behind the stirrups to keep the stirrups in place.

The Rider Prepares for a Lesson

was red in the face. The harder she kicked, the faster he backed. The instructor then pointed out she was holding the curb rein too tight.

At the end of the lesson, each stirrup should be run up the back of the leathers to the top. The leathers are then tucked behind the stirrups to keep them in place.

Your riders gain much by learning to check their tack and adjust their stirrups for themselves. They become conscious of safety features, and are more independent riders.

8

HANDS AND SEATS

The way you teach good hands will either make riders of your class or ruin most of your students. It is quite a trust. A good seat will help greatly to give a rider a polished look. Both are important as they affect the child's control.

A good seat is a relaxed seat. A child should sit erect in her saddle; she should be looking forward between her horse's ears to see where he is going; her legs should be motionless, with the knees bent until only the tip of her toe is visible when she looks over her knee; her heels should be down; her elbows should rest at her sides; her hands should be on either side of the horse's withers, a few inches above them, in a position that feels natural to her. While she is riding, this position should feel comfortable, as well.

The rider's muscles will be developed by riding until this position is natural. You can speed the process by having your classes trot in the trotting position, trot without stirrups, and sit to a slow trot. Simple games such as "Follow-the-Leader" and "Touch Every Fence Post" help the riders to relax. Keep changing the leader and keep the children laughing; the horses will complete the job of making the riders forget their stiffness.

Correct the faults of position you see in your riders. Watch for the child who leans forward apprehensively. An instructor I knew once used praise and criticism well

Hands and Seats 151

A good seat is a relaxed seat.

mixed for one of her students. The instructor said, "While you lean forward that way, you will certainly be ready for anything your horse does. That keeps you right on top of him where you can feel what he is going to do almost before he does it. Of course, it makes you look afraid of your horse, too. The riders who win in horse shows are the ones who sit up straight, looking as confident as can be." The rider remembered to sit straight ever after.

Her advice reminded me of the advice of a gym instructor at Barnard College in the days when Greek Games were a part of the program, and the chariot competition a highlight of Greek Games. I was charioteer for the sophomore class, driving my team of horses, four tall slender girls who did complex steps. I leaned forward in my chariot, eagerly watching over their every move, until the gym instructor took me aside. "No Roman charioteer coddled his horses," she said. "He stood up

A rider's balance is helped by sitting to a slow trot.

in his chariot in a position of command, his head up, his whip raised, and no horse would have dared to step out of line." After that I stood erect. Children need the dominion of a Roman charioteer.

Once in a while you see a rider who leans back when she posts. She rises from the saddle so long after the horse takes his strides that she appears to make him drag his steps. You will have to make her bend so far

Hands and Seats 153

forward she thinks she is leaning forward. Actually, she is sitting up straight, although it does not feel that way to her. She should have a hand's width between her and the back of the saddle.

Often the child who is leaning back also lets her legs slip forward. Be sure her stirrups are not too long before you take any other remedial measure. A child can check the length of her stirrups by standing in her trotting position, her knees silghtly bent. If she is able to take a trotting position without raising her heels or straining to reach her stirrups, her stirrups are the correct length. Show her while she is standing still how hard it is to stand up in the stirrups if her legs are forward. No one can stand if his legs are knocked out from under him. We had an enthusiastic boxer dog at one time. One day, in her eagerness to greet a guest, she raced up behind him. She discovered too late that she could not stop. When she hit him behind the knees with the full force of her thick body, he landed flat on his back.

When a rider's legs slip forward, she loses her balance, too. Shift her legs back; be sure her heels are down. Her heels should also be out to prevent her toes from sticking out. This down and out pressure of the heels forces the muscle inside her thigh against the saddle, locking her on her horse. This "locked on grip" is better than saying, "Grip with your knees." You do not want her to grip with her knees. Rather should she ride with balance. If a rider's toes point out, her knees go out, depriving her of a secure seat.

Sometimes, in her effort to keep her heels down and out, a child will twist her foot on the stirrup so that her weight is resting on the edge of her shoe, not on the ball of her foot. She must rest her foot flat on the stirrup, even if her toes point out when she does. Few children will be able to keep their toes in far enough to have their feet parallel to their horses' sides. As they

If a rider's toes point out, her knees go out, depriving her of a secure seat.

train their ankles by riding, their ankles will become more flexible. The day will come when their heels will be out without an effort, when a sensitive horse will not feel the touch of a foot against his side if one of your riders is on his back.

The rider has a neater appearance if she posts close

Hands and Seats 155

Good hands are resilient, quiet, assured. The reins are long enough to avoid tension on the horse's mouth, but tight enough for the rider to feel the bit.

to her saddle. A girl who stands up until her knees are straight will be rising much higher than necessary to post. You will see daylight between her and the saddle at every step. Let such a rider ride a horse with an easy gait. Her thighs should never leave the saddle, and her seat should only rise a few inches when she posts. You may need to let her bounce without stirrups, then feel how much the horse lifts her when he trots. If she relaxes and lets the horse give her the upward momentum to post, she will stop posting mechanically.

A good seat is much easier to teach than are good hands. Good hands are more important. They are resilient, quiet, assured. A horse knows those hands are there, knows he must obey them, yet is never unnecessarily troubled by them. The reins should be long enough to

The most common fault among intermediate riders is tight reins.

Have your riders work with slack reins until all of them cease to ride with tight reins.

avoid tension on the horse's mouth, but tight enough for the rider to feel the bit.

The most common fault among intermediate riders is tight reins. Have the class work with slack reins part of the time. Teach them that most horses are taught to move more quickly the tighter the reins are.

Some horses seem to attract riders who like tight reins. Fancy Free, a dappled gray Arabian, always prances when held tightly. Her riders smile proudly at being able to hold such an eager horse under control. Instructors are constantly saying, "Give Fancy Free a looser rein, looser, looser." The rider relaxes her grip, Fancy Free stretches her neck happily, and all the prancing goes out of her step.

The reason children keep their reins too short is that they fear they will lose control. Show them again how to shorten reins. The end of the right rein is taken in the left hand, thus freeing the right hand to slide down the right rein toward the horse's mouth. Have the class practice shortening first the right rein, then the left, then both. They should practice until they do it easily, quickly, and quietly. The horse should not feel even the slightest tug on his bit.

Watch for the child who uses strange methods for shortening her reins. She may seize both reins close to her horse's neck. She may twist both reins around her hands or wrists in a deft movement hard for an adult to imitate. Sometimes she simply doubles up the reins in a bunch. Discourage any of these methods.

Sometimes a child will fuss with the reins. Every time the child rides past, you see her flipping the reins around, lifting one hand or the other, or moving her hands as if she could not keep them still. Her problem may be a simple one: she does not know what to do with the bight of the reins. Show her how to place the bight inside her reins on the right side of the horse's neck.

When a rider does not know what to do with the bight of the reins, she tends to move her hands frequently.

The backs of her hands should neither be perpendicular to the ground . . .

nor parallel to it . . .

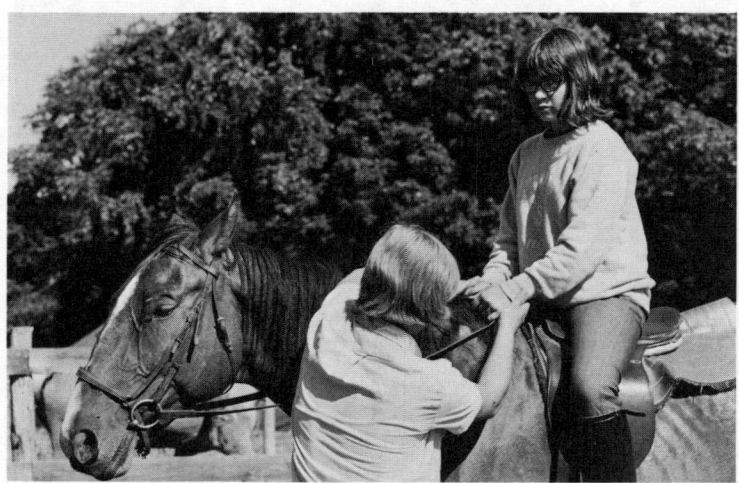

but at an angle between. They should have the same slant as the shoulders of the horse.

A rider who has one rein shorter than the other so that her horse keeps tossing his head or turning it to one side, should be told why her horse is acting strangely.

The position of the rider's hands is also important. The backs of her hands should neither be vertical to the ground nor parallel to it, but at an angle in between. If her hands are straight up and down with her thumbs on top, she has the stiffness of a beginner. If her hands are flat so the palms face the ground, she has no leverage in stopping her horse. Her pull is as weak as if she tried to pick up a bushel of peaches with her hands turned backwards on the handles. Have her rest her hands on the horse's withers. His shoulder blades have the same slant her hands should have when she raises them above the withers again.

Often if a child has her hands flat with the palms down, her elbows will stick out. When she trots, she will

Hands and Seats

If a child holds her hands flat, her elbows may stick out so that you see daylight between her arm and her body.

"fly" with her elbows as if they were wings to be flapped each time she posted. Her arms should rest naturally at her sides, with her elbows bent. However, if she continues to have trouble with flying elbows, have her press her arms against her sides as if hugging herself while she trots around the entire ring.

By means of continuous reminders and days of practice, you will be rewarded at last by one child after another learning how to turn her horse with the touch of a baby finger. For those children who continue to tug on their reins without sympathy for their horses' mouths, suggest they think of their reins as if they were eggs. A brutal tug on an eggshell would burst it in their hands.

It often helps children if you are able to spare an experienced rider to teach on horseback. The experienced rider moves from student to student, teaching by example

The rider with good hands will be able to turn her horse by tightening her lower fingers.

Hands and Seats 165

how to hold reins, how to shorten them, and the correct position of hands. Whenever a mounted instructor is working in the ring, she must be careful not to interfere with the other horses. If she wishes the girl she is helping to trot, she should wait until the entire class is trotting.

While riding a horse beside a child, you can show her with your own light touch on the reins how easily a horse responds if the only pressure he feels means to slow or turn. A child's hands should be so light that they yield to the movement of her horse's head.

You can give the class practice in the correct way to use reins by playing games such as "Red Light." One child stands her horse on the far side of the ring. She counts to 10 and calls a colored light—orange, green, purple, etc. The riders approach as quickly as they can

A game such as "Red Light" gives a class practice in shortening and lengthening reins and turning.

while she counts. If she says "Red light," they must stop. Anyone seen moving must go back to the start. The first horse to reach her wins. As the children try to be the first to pass the girl calling out the numbers and colored lights, yet avoid being caught moving when she calls "Red light," they will constantly be stopping, shortening reins, and being made to turn around to return to the start again.

It will give you a real sense of satisfaction to watch one of your intermediate classes just before the children pass into the advanced ring. The correct riding form, good hands and seat, has given them the tools to make them fine riders. Your satisfaction will be reflected in their faces. Children are delighted to please an instructor they respect. They will feel how well the horses respond when they know the right way to use their bodies and their hands.

III
THE CHALLENGE OF PERFECTION

9

CANTER

The ring of distinction is the advanced ring, or the paddock. A child's face will be alight with pride and excitement when she says, "I passed into the paddock today." It is a day she will always remember. Ahead of her lie riding experiences she has anticipated since her first day on a horse: cantering and jumping.

Plan and explain carefully to your riders where your class will canter the first time. Have the horses stop about 20 feet short of one corner of the ring. One child at a time will walk her horse to the corner. At the corner she will start to canter and continue to canter the entire length of one side of the ring. At the far end, before she turns the next corner, she will stop her horse, a complete standstill stop. Finally, she will walk around the ring to the end of the line of horses. You should stand a short distance from the corner on the side on which the class will be cantering. This gives you a view of that entire side as well as putting you close enough to the corner to speak to each child when she starts to canter.

By using one side of the ring for teaching cantering, the horses learn to take the canter easily, as well as to stop cantering automatically at the end of the ring.

The child who is about to canter for her first time walks toward the corner of the ring. As she walks, she shortens her reins so that she will have control of her horse when he canters. Her horse should be alert,

170   How to Teach Group Riding

In the advanced ring the riders should use the entire ring, keeping as much distance between the horses as possible.

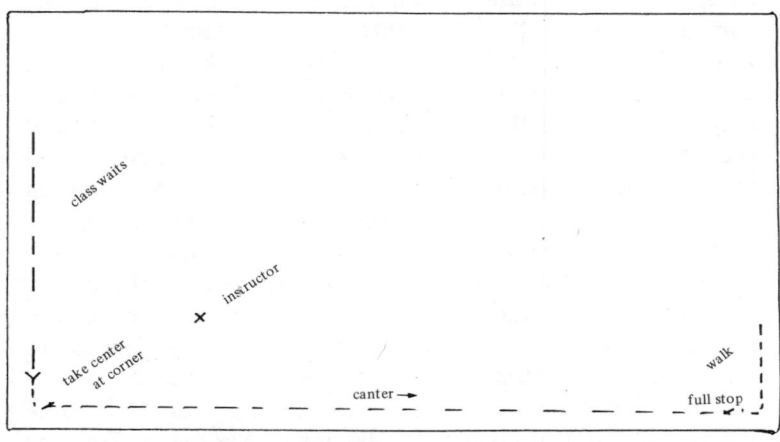

Diagram: Explain to the class where they should canter in the ring, where they should stop.

Canter

expectant. She may need to use leg pressure on both sides to warn him she is going to do something that requires his cooperation. At the corner, she asks for the canter. A horse should canter for leg pressure with her outside leg only.

Unfortunately, few horses will canter with leg pressure alone from an inexperienced rider. The child may need to use her reins. Some horses are trained to canter when the outside rein is lifted at the same time as leg pressure is used. The child needs to raise her hand slightly and give a short tug on the outside rein. Some horses are trained to canter when the inside rein is lifted. A few horses take a canter when both reins are released

Sometimes the only way a child can make her horse canter is to be behind another cantering horse.

suddenly as leg pressure is applied. You know your horses; as each child is ready to canter, tell her which method to use on her horse.

The child should also use her weight, by leaning forward. As soon as her horse canters, she should hold the mane. This keeps her secure until she is balanced at a canter.

Most children have difficulty at first making their horses canter. Encourage them each time they try. After two or three attempts the majority of the class will have cantered once.

The child who cannot make her horse canter should use her heels. She may be riding one of those wise, lazy horses who takes advantage of an inexperienced rider. He must be forced to obey her. Let her use a crop, kick with both feet if she must, and even work on him all the way around the ring until she succeeds.

Sometimes the only way a child is able to make her horse canter is behind another horse that is cantering. Use a more experienced rider to ride the lead horse.

If the child is a weak rider, one who is unable to exact obedience unless her horse is of the cooperative variety, you may need to switch horses for her until she masters the techniques of asking for a canter. Once she has learned how to canter on a horse that canters easily, she will be able to canter on other horses also.

The first time a child canters she is usually so thrilled she forgets to hold the mane, or relax, or do anything you have told her to do. Her horse will probably stop cantering halfway down the side of the ring. The next time she canters remind her to use her legs or her heels to keep him cantering. If she does not feel him slowing down, call out to her to urge him to keep cantering. Do not allow your riders to cluck to their horses to make them canter or to keep them cantering.

If a horse begins to trot after he has started cantering, the child should make him walk before she asks for the

Canter

canter again. She should not try to canter from a fast trot, because she is unbalanced and will not be able to use her hands and legs effectively.

A cantering class should not look like the race track during a race. The children should have quiet, controlled canters. There is a great joy for children in "going fast." However, as soon as a child is able to make her horse canter, she should learn to slow him down so that she has him completely under control.

I once watched with admiration an intermediate class at a well-known stable in Connecticut. The instructor was having the children canter in line. First, he asked for a fast trot. Next, he had everyone pull back on the reins while urging her horse forward with her legs. The horses were so well trained that every horse in line except the last two took a slow "rocking-chair" canter. Before the end of the hour, he had every child in the class doing a collected canter in line.

Once your riders know how to canter, they learn to sit a canter. At first, all of them will bounce at every canter step. One instructor tells her riders to pretend their breeches are glued to the saddle. A rider's hips must give to the motion of the horse when he canters. A hula hula dancer shifts her hips from side to side. A child shifts her hips back and forth, her stomach muscles going in and out, her lower back moving back and forth, as her horse canters. Her hips shift independently of the rest of her body. Her shoulders should not move.

Although the child may still need to lean forward to ask for the canter, as soon as her horse starts to canter, she should sit up straight. An upright position helps her to sit the canter. If she can make herself relax, she will find it easier to sit, too. Usually, only practice will show her the way. If you let her ride different horses while she is learning, she will find one on which she *feels* how to sit. This is a triumph for a rider.

I still remember Queenie, a well-proportioned sorrel

with an easy gait, who was among the horses at the stable where I learned to ride. Although I could make any horse in the stable canter, how to sit a canter defied me. One day the instructor let me ride Queenie. After a trail ride, he allowed the class to canter around a large field that circled the barn and rings. Somewhere in that field I stopped bouncing. It was a wonderful day and Queenie a wonderful horse!

As soon as your riders can sit a canter, they no longer need to hold the mane. Watch that they do not start tugging on the reins instead.

The next step in cantering is learning to take the correct lead. The correct lead in a ring is the one toward the inside. When a horse canters, your riders will see that

Your riders can be taught to tell on which lead a horse is cantering by watching the forelegs of a cantering horse. One shoulder and foreleg reach further forward than the other.

Canter

one of his forelegs reaches farther forward at each step than the other. This is the foreleg on which he leads.

Any child playing horse will pretend to canter by galloping along with one foot always ahead of the other. For many children, playing being a horse is simply imitating the motion of a horse's forelegs. Your riders may have done it, too.

Have your riders watch a horse as it canters until each girl is able to tell on which lead the horse is cantering. Next, as each child canters, have her watch her horse's shoulders until she is able to tell you which one is going farther forward than the other. A child may need to lean way forward until she can see her horse's knees and hooves before she is able to tell on which lead he is.

As soon as a rider knows how to tell which lead her horse has taken, she should be taught to take the correct lead whenever she canters. Ideally, she should be able to time the moment she asks for a canter so that her horse is just about to take a step with the right lead as soon as she uses leg pressure on the outside if he responds as he should.

Inexperienced riders will need to use their legs or their heels on the outside and shift their weight forward at the same time. Because a horse usually takes the correct lead from a corner, let your riders begin learning leads by taking their canters in a corner of the ring.

If a child cannot make her horse take the correct lead from the corner, have her circle her horse and take her canter in the circle.

After your riders are able to take their correct leads in a corner, have them begin to canter halfway along the straight side of the ring. If a child has continuous trouble taking a canter on the correct lead without the help of a corner, show her how to turn her horse toward the fence, then ask for the canter as she shifts him toward the inside. Some horses will only take the correct lead if their heads are turned toward the fence when the riders ask for a canter.

Be sure you do not always work your horses in the same direction. You do not want the horses always using the same lead, nor should the riders only know how to get the lead in one direction.

As soon as your riders know how to get the correct lead, teach them to call out to you each time they canter whether they are on the correct lead or not. Children are so delighted to canter they forget about leads unless you have a routine that makes them remember.

Next, if a rider has the wrong lead, teach her to stop cantering, walk her horse, and then take the canter again. Because you allow your riders to canter for a short distance during the learning process, an incorrect lead is a form of punishment, as it means stopping and starting a second time. For this reason, you will never need to criticize or scold a rider for the wrong lead. You will always be able to encourage and help her to do it right.

Although you have taught your riders to tell leads by the forelegs, a horse should have the correct lead behind, too. Otherwise, he is disunited, or is said to be cross-cantering. This causes a bumpy canter that is difficult to sit. A child should walk her horse and take the canter again if he is disunited.

While you are teaching, only have a few horses canter at a time. Four is about as many as one instructor is able to watch. Keep an eye on those who canter to see that they keep their horses quiet and under control all the way around the ring. Watch for the nervous horse or rider and let that child canter alone. Until your riders are at an advanced level, do not permit prolonged canters by an entire class. Their safety is more important than experience in cantering in a group.

Canter

A skilled rider sits erect when she canters.

The advanced rider should be able to take her canter in the correct lead without bending forward either to make her horse canter or to check her lead. Her seat will be erect throughout the canter. No violent motion of her hands or legs will be visible when she asks for the canter nor when she stops cantering.

She should be able to feel which lead her horse has taken. Almost all horses feel more comfortable on one lead than on the other. A rider learns to tell which her horse is on by the smoothness or roughness of the canter. If in doubt, a downward glance at his shoulders should reassure her. In time, she will know without the downward glance.

Now that your riders know how to make their horses canter, they should learn how to stop a runaway horse. The surest way is to turn the horse in a circle, making the circle smaller and smaller until he is forced to slow down. A rider may need to reach almost to the bit on one side to pull his head around. At the same time, enough pressure should be kept on the other rein to keep the bit from pulling out of his mouth. Sometimes the only way to stop a horse is to brace one hand against his neck, while giving hard, sharp jerks with the other hand. These sudden pulls catch him off balance and either make him turn or stop.

A rider should not give a hard sustained pull to stop a runaway horse. His mouth will become so numb he will no longer feel the bit. If the rider pulls, releases a moment, then pulls again, the horse will feel it. She should also try see-sawing, pulling first one side, then the other on his mouth. Her weight should be kept back, since leaning forward is the signal to most horses to go faster.

My father used to tell the story about a friend of his who could not stop his runaway horse. Every method the man tried failed either to turn or slow the horse. At last, in desperation, he reached forward and grabbed the horse across the nostrils. The horse could not breathe and stopped at once. "How did he ever lean so far forward without falling off?" I used to ask my father. "He had long arms," my father would say. It still seemed to me a very unsafe way to stop a horse.

Riders always think that no horse would ever run away with *them*. In spite of their doubts about the value of the lesson, have them practice how to stop a runaway horse. Pray that it is one lesson they never need to use. It is best of all if you can give them confidence about their ability to stop any horse, "Do not panic," is the first rule in riding. Actually, the danger of a runaway horse is not great in itself. The danger lies in the obstacles that must be avoided. The rider who keeps calm will be able to think faster than the horse and often can guide him to a place where he is forced to stop.

You do not want a runaway horse in class. Whenever a child is unable to control her horse, you must take her off immediately. This is one of the most difficult things to do because the child is so disappointed and discouraged.

Give her a horse on which she can learn what she needs to know to ride the more difficult horse.

Remember, once a class knows how to canter, they still need to practice trotting. It is difficult to close your ears to children's pleas, "Let us canter once more, please." It is time to play a game, then, or begin individual work on positions and control. If you plan your lessons wisely, each period will build to a climax. Then the plea will be, "Let us stay on a few minutes longer, *please*."

10

BEGINNING JUMPING

I had ridden for many years without learning to jump when I decided to take lessons from a prominent instructor. I was assigned to an advanced class. On the first trail ride, as the class cantered through a dense woods, a half-dozen jumps loomed ahead.

I fought to keep down a sense of panic. One of the girls in the class, eager to tell me how much fun I was about to have, said, "Your horse likes to jump as much as he likes oats."

With a frenzied tug, I tried to turn my horse off the path. I might just as well have given him a kick for the response I had. He surged forward, ears pricked.

The horse in front of me sailed across a log that appeared as big as a wall. I called out to the rider behind me, "What do I do?"

"Stand up," came the shouted answer.

I did. In the next few seconds my horse took me over six jumps. He finished the course with his nose on the rump of the horse in front of him. The instructor sat, laughing, on her horse.

"Now you know how to jump," she said.

The hard way, I thought.

The easy way to teach jumping is to prepare your riders for each phase of jumping before anyone goes over a jump-bar. There are two phases in this preparation process. One is the correct position for the rider. The other is the proper motivation of the horse.

Beginning Jumping

Gather the class in a circle around you to explain the procedure. First comes a check for safety. When a rider jumps, her stirrups should be one hole shorter than for normal riding. She should be able to get a finger or two between her body and the top of the pommel so there is no chance of her hitting the saddle when she jumps. As a precautionary measure, she should also check her girth.

The rider takes a trotting position. This is identical to the galloping position, the term that appeals more to advanced riders. Explain that this must be a strong position. She drops her weight into her heels. By bringing her heels down and out, she puts pressure on the inside of her foot, which forces her thigh, knee and lower leg in close to the saddle. Her heels should not be down so far she cannot flex her ankles. She will need to shorten her reins slightly in order to have control of her horse; then she takes the mane about halfway up her horse's neck. This is a secure position. It also prevents her from hurting her horse by snatching on the bit as she jumps.

Explain that when a horse jumps, the rider should always take the galloping position. The momentum of the horse's jump will give her the feeling of being thrust backward in the saddle, but she must not fall down. As his hindquarters go over the jump, if the rider is not high enough out of the saddle, the saddle will hit her in the seat. Though the horse hit her, she will be blamed and told, "You hit your horse."

Have everyone stand in the galloping position. Take each rider by the thigh and give a hard backward pull. The rider should not fall down on the saddle. If she does, either her weight is not into her heels, or her balance is awry. Possibly her legs have slipped forward or she is not holding the mane tightly. Have her sit down in a correct position, her knees bent, her toes just visible when she looks at them over her knee. When she takes her galloping position again, her legs must not move.

After this has been mastered, you are ready to practice

The rider must have a secure galloping position (trotting position) before she is ready to jump.

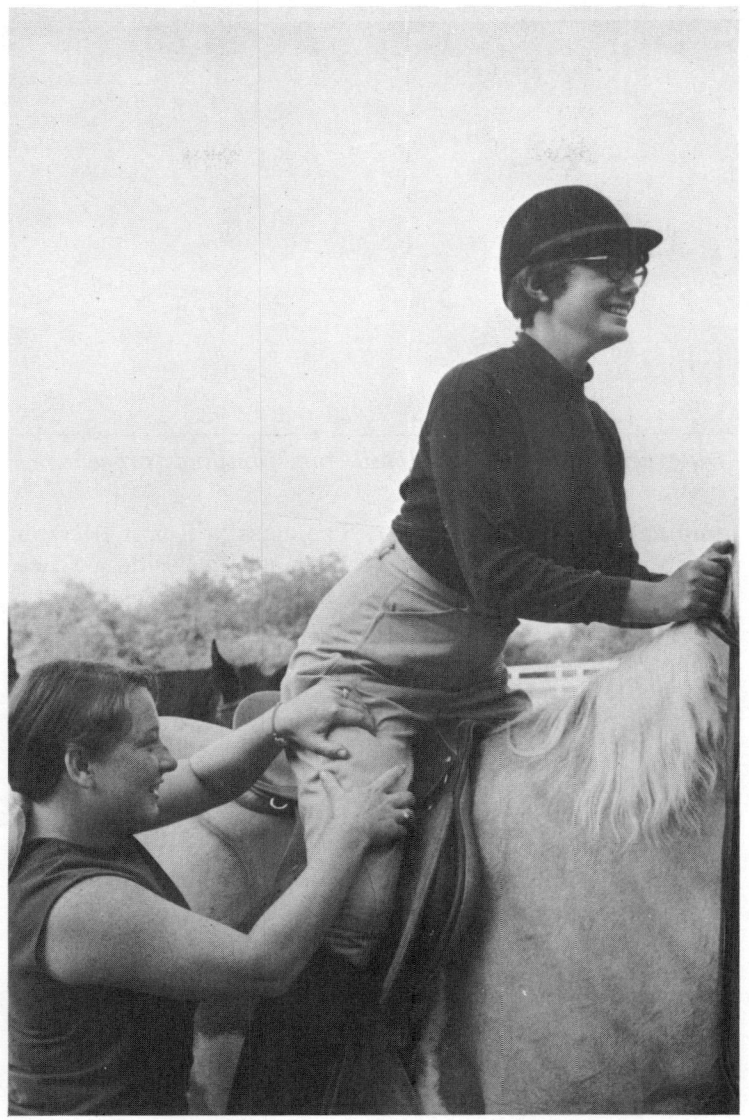

Test her position by tugging on her thigh with both hands. She should not fall back on the saddle.

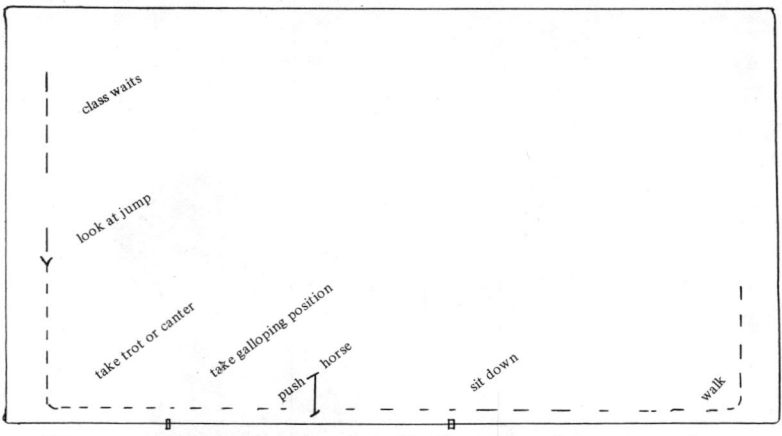

Diagram: Explain in detail the jumping procedure.

jumping without using a bar. The class will trot between two jump standards that have been set up beside a fence. By having the jump next to a fence, the horses are less likely to try to run out on the jump. During the practice jumps your first concern is position. The galloping position should be so natural to your riders before they jump that none of them needs to give it thought when they start jumping. Each time a rider trots over the bar on the ground, correct any mistakes in her position. At the same time, put even more stress on everything she is doing right. Jumping is the most exciting part of riding. Because it is all-important to most riders, it is especially necessary to teach with praise.

Explain in detail the method the rider uses to jump. The jump standards should be set about one-third of the way up a straight side of the ring. About 20 feet before the rider turns the corner, she looks at the jump. This movement of her head warns the horse to look ahead, too. She makes sure her horse goes into the corner. A diagonal approach to a jump indicates lack of control. She trots at a steady pace straight along the fence, her eyes up,

The rider must look at the jump as she approaches it. She must take her horse into the corner to approach the jump directly.

She takes her galloping position before the jump, holds it as she goes over the practice jump with the bar on the ground . . .

and continues to hold it after she has trotted over the bar.

so that her head is up. I have taught jumping in a ring with a big tree at the far end. Sometimes I think the riders must know every branch in that tree, they have been told so often to look at it. A rider's natural inclination is to look down at her hands or the jump. Since her body follows her eyes forward, both she and the horse can be thrown off balance as a result.

The rider takes her galloping position about 15 feet *before* the jump standards. There should be a letter on the fence at this point so the child knows exactly where she should be rising in her saddle. She takes this position so far ahead of the jump to give her practice, and to give *you* a chance to correct her. Long before she reaches the jump, her own position is more likely to be secure.

She remains in the galloping position as she trots between the jump standards and holds it until 15 feet *after* the jump. This shows her the importance of remain-

Beginning Jumping

ing alert after a jump, as well as before it. She keeps her horse trotting at the same steady pace until she reaches the far end of the ring. Before she turns the corner, she makes him walk. Her horse should trot along the fence to avoid any tendency to cut diagonally away from the jump after he has gone between the standards. The child is told the importance of preventing her horse from turning aside after he is over the jump, lest he should stumble or throw her off balance.

The riders will make many mistakes when they practice jumping. Some are due to intense excitement, some to forgetfulness, and a few to ignorance.

A major fault in a rider is heels that go up as she passes between the jump standards. Her safety is involved. She cannot be secure when she jumps with her heels up, because her legs and knees will cease to touch the horse firmly. Never permit a rider to jump a bar until she is able to keep her heels down during her practice jumps.

She must also hold the mane. The mane will keep her secure. It has an added advantage: when she holds it, she cannot jerk on her horse's mouth. Your horses will refuse to jump willingly if they are punished when they jump by having their bits yanked by unbalanced riders.

Horses turn sour on jumping, too, if they are hit by the seats of riders in the middle of the jump. Because of this it is especially important to correct the riders if they sit down after passing between the jump standards. As all instructors know, the "follow through" on the jump is very important.

Watch for the child who looks down as she passes the jump standards. Correct her during the practice jumps, or she will get in the habit of looking back to see if her horse touched the bar, encouraging by such actions the very thing she wants to avoid. Sometimes in a rider's effort to keep her head up and her eyes forward, a child sticks out her chin. This gives her an unnatural and stiff appearance. Occasionally, a rider will tilt her head to one side while she is approaching a jump. This, too, can develop into a habit that prevents her from having a natural, relaxed appearance.

Besides correcting faults in position, correct mistakes in handling the horse. It sounds so simple to have the children trot in their galloping positions along a fence where two jump standards are placed. In practice, they find it difficult because they are saying to themselves, "I'm jumping. I'm jumping."

Your riders will forget to take their horses into the corner before approaching the jump. At this very moment, before they have trotted three steps, they have lost control of their horses. Some of the riders will forget to shorten the reins enough to keep that control. Unless you remind them, most of the riders will let their horses cut the corner after the jump or will stop trotting at a steady pace before the end of the ring.

The girls who trot into the jump with their horses hardly awake will have the most trouble of all making their horses jump a bar. The rider has to work when she jumps or she cannot expect the horse to work.

Practice in trotting and cantering in the galloping position will strengthen the muscles the riders use for jumping. On days when you are not jumping, give the class this practice. If your riders have classes every day, you will probably only have jumping lessons two or three times a week. If the riders only come to learn jumping, practice in the galloping position will be part of the class period.

Make certain every child is wearing a hard hat before going over the bar. First, you raise the bar four inches. Most of the horses will not actually jump four inches, but they will pick their feet up higher as they trot over the bar, which gives the riders their first sensation of jumping.

Beginning Jumping 189

The raised bar demands more of the riders. First, they must kick their horses before the jump. Second, they must stay in their galloping positions when the horse picks up his feet. If a child falls back on the saddle, drop the bar the next time she approaches the jump and have her do a practice jump. This is an automatic system of reward and punishment you will continue to use for all beginning jumpers. Be careful not to add a verbal condemnation to the punishment. Find something to praise instead.

The next step in teaching jumping is to have the riders canter into the jump. Each rider takes her canter at the corner and continues to canter after the jump to the end of the ring. Be sure the riders make their horses alert on the approach. The riders continue to take their galloping positions 15 feet before and hold them 15 feet after the jump.

If you allow a child to jump before she is secure in her galloping position, she will hit her horse on the jump.

Next, you raise the bar to six or eight inches so the horses actually jump.

The first time a child canters over a jump, warn her to hold the mane securely and *stay up*. This final reminder may help her not to hit the horse. Once she feels how hard the backward thrust is when her horse jumps, she will understand why she must be strong in her galloping position. Any child who does not hit her horse on this first jump should receive the praise she deserves.

I felt rather cruel when I took Sue's picture of her first jump with a raised bar. She lost her balance and hit her horse. After the click of the camera, instead of hating me for taking her picture, she managed a smile. This kind of reaction is what makes you love teaching children to ride.

When your riders succeed in making a perfect jump, tell them. Nothing will thrill them more. Never be afraid to praise every detail that is right.

If a horse runs out on the jump, the child needs to see-saw on the reins while she is approaching the jump. She pulls on one rein as she releases on the other, which results in a continuous back and forth motion on the bit. The horse is actually being asked to go first to one side, then to the other, which keeps him so busy he cannot think about running out to one side of the jump.

When a horse does run past the jump on one side, the child should turn him around as quickly as she can and bring him back to take the jump again. Sometimes the horse will run out on a child the second time. She should then circle him so that he reaches a spot about 10 feet in front of the jump when she turns him to face it. She keeps him moving right into the jump. Because his approach is so short, 10 feet, he will not have time to run out.

If the horse refuses the jump, the rider did not push him hard enough during the approach. He must canter

Beginning Jumping

You may need to tell a rider "Now" when she should kick her horse to make him jump.

eagerly. She must use her legs or her heels and a crop on his shoulder if he is lazy. Just before the jump, she must give him a final hard kick so that he knows he has to put an effort into the jump. The rider also needs determination. Unless the rider communicates her will to the horse forcefully, he will not jump. He senses any hesitancy on her part.

If the horse knocks the bar down, the rider did not kick him just before the jump. The next time the girl approaches the jump, tell her, "Now," at the moment when she should kick her horse.

If the rider has done everything correctly but the horse still kicks the bar to the ground, he may be getting bored with the whole affair. Use a four by four for a jump bar, still keeping the jump low. He will not like hitting his legs and will make the effort required to pick up his

Sometimes you may wish to place one side of the bar behind a jump standard to prevent a horse from knocking it down too easily.

The riders wait in line while one horse at a time jumps.

Beginning Jumping 193

feet. You may want to put one side of the bar on the back of one of the jump standards so that it does not fall easily.

Some horses are so eager to jump, they cannot keep calm during the approach. Have the rider walk a horse that is overly eager until she is about five canter steps away from it. Then she releases the reins and lets him canter. She must be careful to give her horse his head going over the jump, so she does not hold him tight all the way. Gradually the rider will learn to control him at a canter for longer distances before the jump. Also, the horse will learn he cannot rush the jump and will gradually become quieter.

It is important to practice beginning jumping over low jumps. By using low jumps you put little strain on the horses. Almost every horse you own will jump an obstacle six or eight inches high. You want your riders to have so much practice that they take their galloping positions naturally and know exactly how to motivate their horses.

The final step in beginning jumping is to teach a rider to take her galloping position only while her horse is jumping. Soon the rider will take her galloping position easily, and hold it perfectly over the jump, as well as afterwards. She will be balanced, she will go over the jump without being jarred, and when the horse lands she will still be standing firmly. Now it is time to teach her how to stand up when her horse takes off, how to sit down when he lands: to "go with her horse." Do not wait any longer than necessary for this step. As long as the child does not hit her horse and has control, she should be allowed to move ahead. The length of time it takes for a rider to be ready for this step varies as much as the length of time it takes for various children to learn to post.

Some riders will be ready to jump a raised bar the first day you teach them the method for jumping. Likewise, some riders will be able to jump with their horses after only one or two lessons in cantering over a raised bar in the galloping position. With a large group of children, arrange the class so that the riders who are jumping four inches are first in line, and those who are ready to jump with their horses are at the end of the line. Always call each rider by name before she starts to approach the jump. This prevents an eager child from getting to the jump before you have time to adjust the bar.

A rider can feel the horse as it rises from the ground. She must learn that this is when she rises from the saddle. The horse gives the rider an upward thrust as if he were pushing her from the saddle. Just as a horse lifts his rider to post, so he helps her to rise from the saddle as he jumps. The horse should be cantering, not trotting, when a child is learning to jump with her horse, because the upward thrust can be felt more easily at a canter. If the rider pushes herself forward, instead of leaving it to the horse, she can throw the horse off stride and cause him to miss his timing on the jump. You can help a child with her timing by telling her during her approach, "Wait, wait, *now*."

Do not have her sit down with her horse until she has perfect timing on her take off. You can wait several days before teaching her when to sit down.

The rider should sit down immediately after her horse's hind feet touch the ground. If she sits down before his feet touch the ground, she hits the saddle. This can throw him off stride or even make him hit the jump with his hind legs. If she stays up too long, not only does she appear to be holding her galloping position too long, she is not in a position to keep her horse under the kind of control she will need when she is jumping more than a single jump. Only by practicing again and again and being told each time she jumps whether her timing is right or wrong will she get the feel for it.

The last step in beginning jumping.

(1) A rider needs to rise from the saddle just as the horse takes off . . .

(2) to stay out of the saddle over the jump . . .

(3) and to sink back into it after the jump, sitting down after the horse's hind feet have touched the ground.

When the rider sits down, she must not collapse on the horse. She should sink down into the saddle, her knees and ankles flexed-in to absorb the shock of landing. The sensation is almost the same as if the rider had jumped the bar herself and landed on the ground. She would bend her knees to absorb the shock of hitting the earth. If she were to land with stiff legs, the shock would be much greater. If her legs are stiff when jumping, she will give both her horse and herself a shock.

If a child loses her balance when she rises from the saddle or hits her horse before he lands, have her continue practicing with her galloping position on the jump for a few more days. If she cannot concentrate on control and jumping with her horse at the same time, postpone learning how to jump with her horse until she is effective with her control. A rider must have absolute control of her horse to jump well.

11

ADVANCED JUMPING

Low jumps cease to be a challenge when a rider can take them every time with ease. As your confidence in your riders' ability increases, you dare to raise the bar higher. Three-and-a-half feet is as high as you need to raise it while you are teaching group riding. Any child who is able to jump three-and-a-half feet correctly should be able to jump any height. The lower the bar, the more jumps each horse can take in a day and the more practice your riders can have. The rider's eagerness to learn should be coupled with determination.

A well-known instructor used to ask a rider before the jump was raised, "Well, do you feel brave today?" If the rider said, "No, not exactly," the instructor did not raise the bar. The rider, as well as the instructor, must be confident if the jump is to be higher than a couple of feet.

Timing becomes more important as the jump bar is raised. After a child has jumped a horse a few times, she will feel how he has to stretch for the jump if he is too far away with his last stride. She will also feel how cramped his last step must be if he has come too close to the jump before taking off. In this case, he often hesitates a moment before springing over the bar. If the rider is with her horse, she will rise when he does in both cases. However, if he has not timed the jump correctly, he is likely to kick the bar or knock it off completely.

Only a great deal of practice will teach a rider to tell

whether her horse will take the jump in his stride or not. Until she can tell that, she cannot correct the length of his stride. Usually, a rider learns to tell about three strides before jumps whether her horse will stretch for the jump or needs a short extra step at the last moment. She needs to know about five or six strides before the jump, so she can correct him before it is too late.

She can practice cantering over a bar on the ground and trying to gauge her horse's steps so that he will go over the bar without changing his stride at the last moment. One instructor used to place a quarter on the path in the ring and have her riders try to make their horses stop on it with a right forefoot. To lengthen the horse's stride, the rider squeezes with her legs as the horse starts each stride. To shorten his stride, the rider pulls him back just as he comes down from one step and is about to surge forward for the next.

A rider who is determined to jump a higher jump and is able to time her horse's stride to some extent, also needs to know how to make her horse jump the raised bar. Now is the time to teach her how to punish a horse by using a crop behind her leg, or on the horse's flank. If her horse refuses the jump, she should stand him in front of it and hit him hard once or twice with the crop.

As she is coming into the jump, she should be able to sense if her horse is hesitant or considering a refusal. A reminder with the crop on his flank at the same time as she kicks him may make up his mind for him, so that he jumps. Whatever it takes to make him jump, the rider should be willing to give it to him.

An advanced rider, asked to describe what was important in jumping, said, "The approach is the whole jump, really. You know when your horse is going to take off well. You feel him with your seat and you feel him in your hands. Then you can go with him."

Your riders should learn to jump an in and out almost

Advanced Jumping 199

On an in and out the rider must be thinking of the second jump as she clears the first one.

as soon as they learn to jump higher than a couple of feet. The first time you set up a second jump, place it far enough away from the first one to give your riders time to think in between.

The rider should be looking ahead to the next jump even as she is coming down from the first jump, before her horse's feet touch the sod. As her horse hits the

No matter what happened on the first jump, she collects her horse and prepares to push him for . . .

the second jump.

ground, she collects him enough to let him know she is guiding him. She must have him under control. If she has been thinking ahead rather than thinking about how she did on the first jump, she will be prepared to take the next jump with her horse. She must use leg pressure, or her heels and the crop, for the second jump just as she did for the first one.

If her horse runs out between the jumps, she lost control. She should bring him back between the jumps, make him take the second jump alone, then repeat both jumps together.

The next step is to place the in and out with about two canter steps between the jumps. Keep both jumps low at first. Your riders will now need to think about two jumps before approaching, rather than preparing first for one, then for the other.

When a rider is able to jump an in and out with two steps in-between, narrow the distance to make only a single stride between them. This means that as soon as the horse comes down, he must take off again. The rider should not come all the way down into her saddle between the jumps. She should lean forward to prepare for the horse taking off again.

The position of a rider's hands will change as she becomes more proficient at jumping. As a beginner she held the mane. The next step is to use a bridge with the reins. A rider bridges her reins by taking both reins crossed so that she is holding the end of her right rein, as well as her left rein, in her left hand, and the end of the left rein with the right rein in her right hand. She rests the bridge across his neck to help her keep her balance and prevent her from falling forward on the horse. Sometimes it is easier to control a horse with half a bridge, with just one rein crossed through the opposite hand.

As the rider gains experience jumping, she should depend less and less on the bridge of her reins. Have her

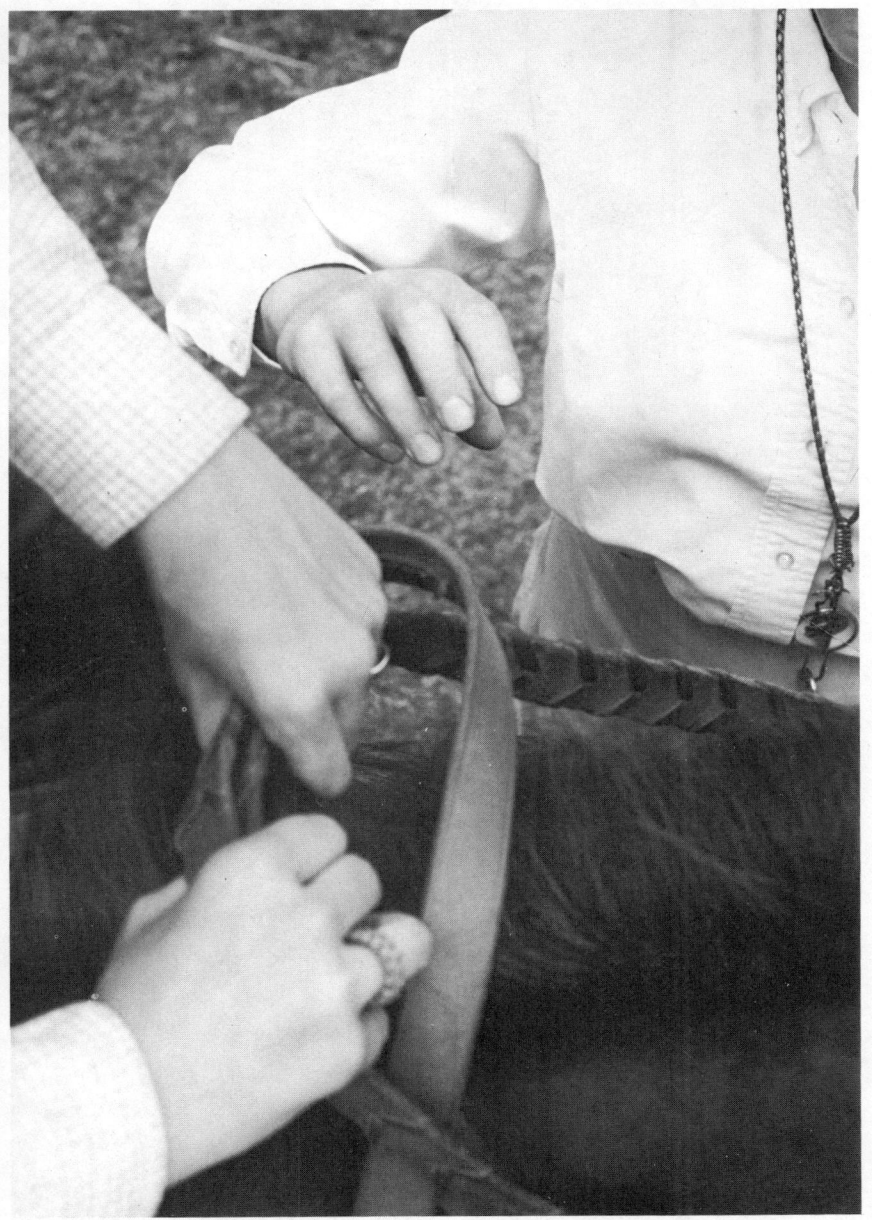

The rider next learns to jump with a bridge; each rein is crossed through both hands.

The bridge is rested against the horse's neck to help the rider keep her balance as she jumps.

In the most advanced position of the hands, the rider moves her hands forward and down with the movement of the horse's head.

practice cantering in her galloping position without touching the horse with her hands. As she learns to balance more easily, she will not need to put weight on the bridge when she jumps. Next she may jump with her hands resting on either side of her horse's neck.

Finally, the rider will be able to "follow through" with her hands. When a horse jumps, he stretches his head forward and also lowers it in relation to the rest of his body. A rider should learn to feel this movement. Her hands should reach forward and drop lower on the horse's neck at the same time. It is a progressive movement, becoming accentuated as the horse is in the air, then returning to normal as the horse reaches the ground. The pull of his head makes her yield with her hands; otherwise she would jerk the reins. If she follows through correctly,

If the rider's hands are correct, you will visualize a straight line from the bit to her elbow as she rises for the jump . . .

Advanced Jumping

and as she goes over it.

there will be a straight line from the bit to her elbow during the jump. The straight line is not what is important, but rather how she moves her hands in response to the movement of her horse.

If a child snatches at her horse's mouth in the middle of her jump, have her use the bridge until she is better balanced. This is the surest way to help her and protect the horse.

A child may have hard hands which are insensitive to the bit. Before she tries to follow through with her hands on a jump in a mechanical imitation of the correct position, she needs to work hard on her hands. She should develop quiet, resilient hands that will feel and yield to the motion of a horse's head even at a walk.

One way you can help your riders to feel the movement of a horse on a jump is to set up a row of four low jumps between two barriers. The fence may serve as a barrier on one side; a set of wings may be used as a fence

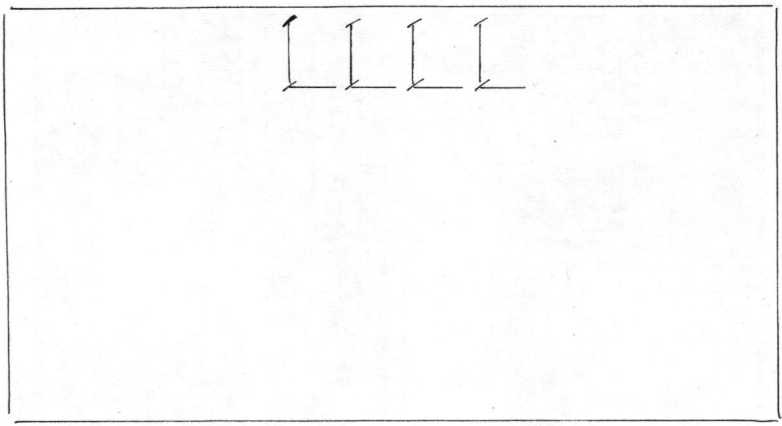

(Diagram) Four low jumps in a row between two barriers help a rider feel the movement of a horse's head when he jumps, as well as how to time herself for jumps.

on the other side. The rider will not need to think much about controlling her horse and can catch a feeling of the rhythm of his movement as he goes up and down for each jump.

Continue to correct any faults that develop in a child's position when you allow her to go over higher jumps or an in and out. If she begins to fly out of the saddle on higher jumps, she is forgetting to push her heels down and out, to keep her weight forward and her thighs and knees against the saddle.

The greater the variety of jumps to which a rider is exposed as she progresses, the better experience she gains and the better it is for her horse. The rider is also helped by riding many different horses. They present a diversity of problems so she learns how to deal with anything she encounters.

You may add a brush jump for variety. A spread jump is also a challenge. The rider goes over a spread

A spread jump is a challenge.

jump the same way as any other post and rail jump, except she stays out of the saddle a little longer.

One camp used a series of long wooden boxes painted various colors. Each box was about a foot high and three feet long. They could be stacked to make walls or a low solid jump. One rider was so afraid of any new type of jump she was afraid to try going over those boxes even when they were only a foot high.

Either the horse, or the rider, or both, will do something wrong on every new jump. After two or three exposures, however, the jump becomes routine.

The chicken coop is one of the most difficult jumps for your riders. It looks so solid that it has a frightening effect on the rider and sometimes on the horse, as well. My daughter described her first encounter with a chicken coop in a class in a horse show at the County Fair. The coop was the second jump. "When I saw it there ahead of me," she said, "it looked like a huge towering wall that covered half the ring. I was almost relieved when Decision refused it."

A horse follows the same path in the air for jumping a chicken coop as he does for a post and rail jump. Only the appearance makes it more difficult.

Solid jumps, such as walls, are easier to jump in one respect. The horse will clear them. He may refuse or run out, but if he jumps, he is unlikely to kick the top.

An outside jump course in a field or woods gives great pleasure to your riders. They discover how much more difficult it is to control their horses in the open than in a ring. They also have a wonderful feeling of triumph when they succeed. It is important that the riders learn to keep their horses in slow canters between jumps so that they have them under perfect control all the way around the course. They must remember to push their horses for every jump just as they do in the ring.

When I was watching my daughter learn to ride, I

The chicken coop, which looks so solid, is one of the most difficult jumps for your riders.

Your advanced riders will enjoy a jump course in a field or woods more than any other ride.

Advanced Jumping

discovered that the change from a beginning rider to an advanced one came when she learned to jump any kind of jump placed in front of her horse. The battles she had making him turn into the jump, approach it without weaving, and go over it without protest, turned her into a forceful rider. Until a rider is able to insist on obedience from her horse, she will never be in an advanced class. If, in the process of demanding obedience, she becomes cruel or misuses her hands, she will be a failure.

You will know your riders have reached the advanced stage when they can take an unusual jump with equilibrium. One day I saw a young girl set up three picnic benches on top of each other in the middle of an open field. She turned her horse toward them and he jumped them eagerly without a glance at the open spaces on either side. Both horse and rider were happy jumping. This is a joy to see.

12

THE SKILLED RIDER

The skilled rider is one who not only makes her horse do anything she wants but looks well while she is doing it. By giving your riders new experiences on horseback, you help them to demand of their horses all the horses are capable of giving.

There are many skills a rider can develop at a trot. You have already had her practice trotting without her stirrups in an effort to develop her muscles and to help her be balanced under all circumstances. She should learn to post without her stirrups as well. Most riders find it easier to post without stirrups than to bounce without them. A child will need to brace her knees slightly higher than normal on the saddle when she starts posting without her stirrups. When she is not posting, however, she should let her legs dangle, her toes dropped, in a comfortable position. This relaxed position is actually a more secure one than holding her feet and legs as if she had invisible stirrups.

Advanced riders should know three speeds of the trot; slow, normal, fast. The rider sits to the slow trot. The rider should make her horse take a normal trot before she stops him after he has been doing a slow trot. Otherwise, when he is trotting slowly for her, he will think he is slowing down to stop.

The normal trot is a smooth, even gait, in which the horse is neither hurrying nor slowing his steps. The rider

A rider's balance improves until she is able to post easily without stirrups.

The rider sits to a slow trot.

In an extended trot the rider can see her horse thrust his forelegs further forward. He also raises them higher than in a normal trot.

The Skilled Rider

must make the horse stay in a normal trot; he will not do it automatically.

The fast trot, or extended trot, is a quick trot in which the horse lifts his legs higher and appears to the rider to thrust his forelegs so far ahead as to nearly straighten his knees. The rider urges her horse into an extended trot by squeezing with her legs while she is in the saddle after she posts for each step. The rider should feel in her hands whether the horse is about to canter, and prevent him with just enough tension on the reins.

In the ring the horse should only be asked for a fast trot on the straight sides of the ring. He should be slowed to a normal trot around the corners.

In the advanced ring you should teach the emergency dismount at a trot. If a child is able to jump off a horse easily and correctly at a trot, she can also do it at a canter. It is usually better not to practice the emergency dismount at a canter with a group of children. Children are not careful of themselves and fly off their horses at a canter as if the horses were standing still. The ground always meets them with too much of a jolt.

The emergency dismount is the same at any gait. The most important thing to watch is that children kick their feet out of their stirrups before starting to grab the horse around the neck to jump off. An experienced rider should be able to catch the right rein with her left hand when she reaches under the horse's neck with both arms. If she can do this as she is dismounting quickly, she will have a secure enough hold on her horse to swing on his neck until he stops. A rider should break her leap with one elbow still across the horse's neck when she lands. Be sure your riders land facing the front of their horses and take a few running steps until their horses stop trotting. The riders should also be conscious of keeping a firm hold on the reins in order to stop their horses and to prevent them from running away.

An advanced rider should be able to catch her left rein with her right hand when both arms encircle the horse's neck in an emergency dismount.

The Skilled Rider

One girl who had learned to make an emergency dismount called several months later to tell how her horse had run away with her in a park. She was so frightened she could not figure out what to do to stop him. Suddenly she realized the horse was racing straight toward a busy avenue. The cars were whizzing back and forth in front of her. As the horse reached the street, she did an emergency dismount. "It wasn't a very good one," she admitted, "but I landed all right." The horse bolted through the traffic. He wheeled and ran and cars dodged. Though he reached the other side without being hit, the child would probably have fallen off had she tried to stay with him. She said triumphantly, "The emergency dismount saved my life."

Your riders should also learn how to trot a figure eight correctly. A method that works well is to take one horse by the bridle. Lead him into the center of the ring and explain when you stop you are standing in the middle of the eight. The middle is the place a rider begins and stops trotting her figure eight. Lead the horse in a large circle and return to the center; then lead him in a circle for the second loop of the eight in the other direction. Have the child walk her horse around the figure until she knows exactly where she should trot.

Since a rider should post on the outside diagonal, each time she passes the center of her figure eight and changes directions to make the next loop, she should change diagonals. She may change diagonals either by sitting for an extra bounce or standing for a moment until she can pick up the other diagonal.

An advanced rider should be able to keep her horse at a steady gait. If she is trotting a figure eight, her circles should be round, her gait smooth and unbroken by hesitation, or by her horse slowing down or hurrying. If she is doing any one of the three speeds of a trot, the horse's gait should be unvaried.

The advanced rider should no longer need to look at her horse's shoulder by bending forward to see if she is posting on the correct diagonal, or to check if she has changed diagonals correctly. She should be able to feel how her horse is moving. She will find it easier to post on one of his diagonals than the other, just as it is easier to canter on one lead than on the other. By knowing which diagonal is more comfortable she has a guide to help her tell on which diagonal she is posting. She can take a quick look, too, without altering her position.

After a rider has learned to trot a figure eight, she should learn to canter one. At first she should canter in large circles. As she becomes more adept, she can make her circles smaller. Some horses are more willing than others to canter and take either lead, and they can be cantered in small figure eights.

The rider begins cantering at the center of her eight. She decides which direction she will go and takes the inside lead for that circle. When she returns to the center of the eight again, she should take two or three trotting steps. Next, she takes the other lead for the opposite direction. She finishes her eight by standing still in the center.

You may want her to back her horse then. He should back several steps in a straight line. She should remember to use her legs in front of the girth while she is asking him to back with her hands.

Advanced riders should also know controlled backing. The horse should be made to back only a single step at a time, then another, then another. The rider puts pressure on her reins to ask the horse to back. As soon as she feels him yield, she releases. He should take only one step with one foot. Again she asks him to back, and releases the instant she feels him begin to obey. She should back five or six steps in this manner.

A rider should know how to take a lead when she is

The rider should be able to pick up one lead as she begins to canter in a straight line across the ring . . .

in the center of her straight line, she trots a few steps . . .

going in a straight line across the center of the ring. The rider will pick up one lead as she starts across the center of the ring. In the middle of the line, she should trot a few steps, then take the opposite lead while still cantering in a straight line.

If a rider has difficulty changing leads in her figure eight, she should be shown again how to use her weight toward the inside of the turn when she applies leg pressure on the outside. She may use one rein to lift his head, too, if her horse responds to this aid. However, until she is able to take either lead in a figure eight, she should not be asked to change leads in a straight line.

A rider should be decisive when she is working with a horse. She should not begin a figure eight, for example, see which lead her horse takes, and then circle in that direction. She must make up her mind where she is going, which lead she will take, and then be sure the horse obeys.

then takes the other lead.

The Skilled Rider

A rider takes her galloping position when doing a hand gallop.

An instructor should be able to knock away the stirrup of an advanced rider without the rider losing her balance at a walk, a trot, or a canter.

The Skilled Rider

Advanced riders enjoy a hand gallop. The rider should take her galloping position. The horse should begin with a canter, on the correct lead. The rider should have her reins short enough for control; when she reaches forward, there should be no tension in the reins. It is safest to allow only one child to gallop at a time.

Your riders should ride with correct form, no matter how confident they become. They need a great deal of practice to become excellent riders. Discourage sloppiness, such as riding with one hand while chatting with a friend on the horse behind, or slouching in the saddle, or tucking one foot across the front of the saddle as if riding side saddle. The unwary rider is likely to be jolted into alertness in an unpleasant way.

Your riders have not outgrown the need for stirrups, but they do not need to keep their heels as far down as they did as beginners. They will flex their ankles more easily. If an instructor knocks away one of a rider's stirrups, she will not become unbalanced because she lost it.

A game puts a spark into an advanced class, just as it does into an intermediate one. Relays, tag, walking and trotting races are always exciting. One game that is adaptable only to the advanced ring is "War." This is a team game. It is easiest on the horses if halters are used over the bridles. The object of the game is to capture either horses or riders from the opposite team. Each side sends out a champion first. The two competitors try to lead each other's horses back to home base, or pull a rider across the home line. A rider may dismount if she wishes. A team may have three or four riders work together against the same number from the opposite team. You need to be an unbiased referee for this game.

Although you teach your riders everything they might be expected to do in a horse show, they will be competent riders only if they are as courteous and have as much control of their horses outside the ring as they do inside

Riding should be a happy time with moments of play and laughter the riders will remember all their lives.

it. The discipline of the advanced ring may be relaxed at times, as long as the rules for safety are obeyed. Riding should be a happy time, with moments of play and laughter the riders will remember all their lives.

IV
READY TO RIDE ANYWHERE

13

HAPPINESS WITH HORSES

Riders who are given the opportunity to ride on trail, to ride bareback, and work their horses together as a unit, will have a full riding program.

Trail rides should be for everyone, even beginners. They can go on trail safely if you send a companion with each horse. The companion may only need to walk along, keeping a wary eye on the horse beside her. Some of the horses that are a bit eager will need to be led. An experienced rider on horseback should lead the trail, just as they lead intermediate and advanced trail rides. Of course, for beginners, you need an especially safe trail. A woods near the ring is ideal. It must be an area without traffic.

The companions accompanying riders on a beginning trail need to be alert. An inexperienced rider cannot be depended upon to react quickly to the unexpected. Lady, one of our horses, became quite dependable for beginners in her old age, none of her Arab spirit showing as she trotted around the beginners' ring. She appeared more content with beginners than with advanced riders who had ridden her formerly. The advanced girls were always asking her to jump when she had made it clear she had no intention of going over a bar. One day, after a beginning trail ride had been gone for about 15 minutes, one of the "companions" came rushing back to the ring. Her breath was coming so fast she could hardly speak. "Janie fell off," she said.

Even beginners can take a trail ride if a "companion" walks with every horse.

"What happened?" the instructor asked.

"Lady jumped a log," the child said, "but Janie's all right."

The other horses had stepped sedately over the log. Not Lady. Perhaps she remembered the glorious days in the paddock when she used to jump. Perhaps she only wanted to please the little girl who rode her. Lady had

Happiness with Horses

not hurried about it; she simply popped over the log while she was walking. That was Lady's last trail ride with beginners.

The safest kind of trail ride for intermediates is a small one. One camp found it a very successful procedure to send two intermediate riders and an instructor on a trail every riding hour. The frequency of these trail rides made the intermediate ring extremely popular. Actually, it benefited the camp in this use of the horses. They had chosen three horses that could not be used well in any other way. Red was used for lead because she was a stubborn mare who refused to learn aids. White Light was a pretty horse in the children's opinion, but she only had one gait she would take for a child: a walk. The third horse, Spook, was antisocial in a ring. There he would lay his ears flat even if the closest horse were across the ring. On trail, he was a gentleman. The instructors traded hours

Trails for advanced riders may be large or small, but more instructors are needed for the larger groups.

in the intermediate ring so that each one had an hour leading the two-horse trail. They enjoyed it as much as the children did.

Trails for advanced riders can be large or small. If there are more than five horses, an experienced rider should bring up the rear because the instructor who is leading cannot keep an eye on that many horses behind her. If you have 15 or 20 horses on a trail ride, instructors should be spaced throughout the line. The riders can be given individual instruction on trail rides if you can spare an instructor to ride up and down the line, riding in pairs first with one child, then with another, and teaching as she rides.

Be sure you test the advanced horses on trail before children ride them. A horse may be safe in the ring but cannot be held by a child on trail. Avoid taking horses on trails which must be ridden bareback. Unless your riders are very adept they are safer with saddles.

Take care, too, in choosing the horse each rider uses. If you are not certain a child will have control of a horse, do not gamble if she is to ride him on trail. Either leave her behind in the safety of the ring, or find a different horse for her. The chances are nothing will happen at all on the trail ride, but be prepared for the unexpected. Once, when I had a group of nine-year-old girls out on trail, I felt everyone would be safe if we only walked. We were on two hundred acres of "no-man's land," on which I had never met anyone on foot. Suddenly, so close that the sound seemed in our ears, a gun shot rang out. As I whirled my horse to block the line, two horses crashed through the trees and disappeared far down the trail. Close on their heels was a riderless horse. Visions of the two girls being thrown in some far off spot, or being lost in the wilderness, mingled with the specter of some terrible accident behind me. What had happened to the rider for that riderless horse?

A note of warning, given pleasantly, is an important procedure before a trail ride begins.

Just then the child who had fallen off shoved her way past the other horses who stood quietly, now that silence spread through the woods. "I lost my glasses," she said.

If that was the worst of her worries, she could not be hurt much, I thought with relief. A few minutes later, the two girls whose horses had bolted by came back, still mounted, leading the horse of the girl who had lost her glasses.

"How did you stop them?" I asked.

"They all stopped by themselves to eat grass in a field," the girls answered in a chorus. It seemed a minor miracle.

Before you leave on a trail ride, explain the important things the riders should remember. The riders should mount and dismount inside the ring before and after the trail ride. Each rider should keep her distance; she should be able to see the heels of the horse in front of her when she looks over her horse's ears, just as she did in the line in the beginners' ring. The last horse in line should keep up with the others, not lag as much as possible in order to have a private canter to catch up.

If you are to ride beside roads, the riders should keep their horses off the pavement. The pavement is more slippery than the shoulder and it is harder on horses' feet. When you wish to cross a road, the horses should all line up on one side facing the street. At a signal from the leader, everyone takes her horse across the street at the same time. If a noisy vehicle approaches, or if the horses must pass anything scary, the horses should be made to face the vehicle or object so they can examine it and decide that it will not hurt them. Things which approach from the rear appear strange to horses.

You may need to cross a creek. Be sure the horses walk briskly so they do not try to lie down and roll in the water. One of my most embarrassing moments occurred in a creek. I had brought a large group of children to the creek on horseback. As we rode into the water, I said, "Be sure you do not let your horses roll. Keep their heads up." The words were barely out of my mouth before my horse put his head down. I could not get it up fast enough. A moment later he was down and I was standing knee-deep in the creek.

Trail rides through wooded countrysides are always pleasant but involve problems, too. A rider must remember to let branches slip past her body. If she takes hold of a branch until she is past it, then lets go, it will snap sharply against the next rider in line.

Do not allow your riders to canter up or down hills. Even on a slight downward grade a horse can lose his balance on a small stone and, because of the grade, he can fall. A wise old horse-trader used to say, "It is the ups and downs that ruin horses' legs. Keep your horses in your nice flat rings and you'll never have lame horses." It is, however, what you make the horses do on the ups and downs that is most important.

A rider should let branches slip past her body so they do not snap in the face of the rider behind.

When a horse is going up hill, the rider should take his trotting position to free the horse's hindquarters. Have the riders watch the horses in front of them. They will see how the horses use their hindquarters for balance and climbing. When going down a hill, the horse braces himself with his hindquarters to keep from slipping, but he picks his way very carefully with his front legs. The rider's weight should not be forward; it makes it even more difficult for the horse to balance with his forelegs.

The riders should alternate the diagonals on which they post, because it is better for the horse if his riders do not always post on the same diagonal. Leads should be alternated as well.

Before leaving on trail rides, remind your riders again of the various methods of stopping a runaway horse. They can circle a horse, making smaller and smaller circles until he is forced to slow down. They can also brace themselves against his neck with one hand and give hard sharp pulls on one rein with the other hand.

On trail at the command, "ALL STOP," the riders should stop their horses immediately, just as they do in the ring. If one child is having trouble with her horse, the other riders will not become involved if they are standing still. It encourages the troublesome horse to give his action a second thought. Horses feel more secure if following the mob.

The instructor who leads the trail should be conscious every minute of what the riders are doing. Before she trots, she makes sure the entire line is on even ground where it is safe to trot. After she comes down a hill, she waits until everyone else is down the hill, too, before changing gaits. If the ground is muddy in one area, the lead rider is careful to walk or skirt the area when possible. The riders should not canter or trot through mud on trail anymore than they would in a ring, lest their horses slip and fall.

A hunt day in the woods, with stuffed animals in the trees, is always popular.

Even on trail rides an instructor needs to be conscious of the ways to make riding fun. As a rule she should not use the same type of games that are played in the ring. The children are more excited on trail; so are the horses. Furthermore, there are no boundaries to help keep the horses under control when children are on trail.

Keep looking for new trails, new views, a different approach. Picnic rides and overnight rides add zest to your program. A hunt day in the woods is always popular. Stuffed animals or paper ones are hidden the night before throughout the woods. The animals can be reached on horseback although some are not only difficult to reach but difficult to find. The advanced riders, divided into teams, hunt in groups. The team which brings home the most animals wins.

New trails can be blazed to criss-cross old ones. One riding instructor I knew had a reputation for exciting trails, because she always blazed new ones. She took my husband and a friend on one of her famous trail rides once. The ride enhanced her reputation. While blazing a trail along the top of a ravine, she ducked under a fallen tree. My husband watched her lean down along the side of her horse's neck so the tree trunk would not scrape her back.

"I'm not leaning out over any ravine," he said to himself, and grabbed his horse around the neck instead. Although he crouched as close to the saddle as he could, the tree trunk ripped the shirt off his back.

His friend, behind him, did not like either alternative. The ravine looked steep and he was not going to scratch *his* back.

The instructor heard him shout. She stopped and looked back hurriedly. The man's horse was in line where it ought to be, but not the man. My husband's friend was swinging on the tree trunk, which he hugged with both arms while his legs dangled over the edge of the ravine.

If you save bareback for rainy days, your riding program is always exciting.

Stirrup Tag is fun on a rainy day.

For children, it is almost as much fun to ride bareback as to go on a trail ride. If you keep bareback for special occasions, such as rainy days, and horses with girth sores or other cuts that prevent them from having a saddle, bareback is a real blessing to a riding program. Horses without saddles are very popular under these circumstances. Often a horse with a sharp backbone that would ordinarily be ridden only if he had a saddle, will have an eager rider on his back. Thanks to bareback riding, you will find it possible to ride in the rain. Some of the happiest classes of all will be on days when the sky is dropping mist. No saddles to saddle-soap afterward, either. The right approach to rainy days will make your riders look forward to them with anticipation. Younger children, however, unless they are in the advanced ring, should ride with saddles even on rainy days. They do not mind the rain and will be happy just to be on horses.

Games at a walk keep the class interesting if the ground is too wet to go faster. Walking relays, "Snatch the Bacon," "Musical Chairs," "Stirrup Tag" and drills are good standbys.

Until a child is well-balanced bareback, she slips off more easily than if she were on a saddle. During the learning period, encourage your riders to hold the mane. Tell them to keep their horses at a slow trot when they are trotting, because it is easier to stay on. Many will post when they trot; a child needs to bring her knees up slightly on the horse if she wants to post bareback. When children are learning to canter, they should hold the mane, until they can make their horses take a canter from a walk and are balanced at any gait. Once your riders have reached an advanced status and know how to canter well with a saddle, you can lift the restrictions on bareback riding. Insist, however, that if a child rides without a saddle during a regular class period, she resaddles her horse for the next rider.

A rider should hold the mane when she learns to canter bareback.

The easiest way to mount bareback is to be given a leg up. Some horses can only be mounted bareback in this manner. A few riders will be able to swing onto a horse by seizing a fistful of mane and tossing one leg over his back as they jump, as cowboys do sometimes in the movies. If the horse will stand quietly, the rider may be able to put one hand on his mane, the other on his back, jump and catch him with her elbows on the other side so she can swing a leg across his back. A rider should not come racing at her horse from the side, leap and land across his back. The horse may be startled into leaping, too.

The other way a child can mount bareback is to take her horse to a fence, the slope of a hill, a log or a rock. By standing on something beside her horse she will be able to mount easily. Children should practice mounting in

The easiest way to mount bareback is a leg up, but some children are able to vault onto a horse without startling him.

this manner with a saddle, too, in case they need to mount when they are alone sometime and cannot reach the stirrup from the ground.

A varsity team, made up of four, eight or more riders, gives status to the riders chosen and also drills them in precision. In addition, the riders have the pleasure of working together with horses as a unit. Begin with the simple figures used in a grand march, riding in twos, fours, eights and splitting up again. Try to keep the horses who work well together as pairs. This type of

A varsity team gives status to the riders and drills them in precision with their horses.

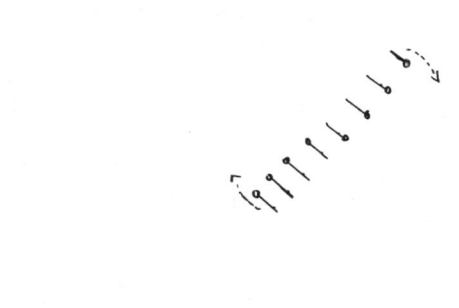

(Diagram) To form a wheel four horses face one direction, four the opposite direction, all eight in a straight line. The two center horses pivot as the others move forward around them.

work, however, often teaches the horses to cooperate, too, or at least to tolerate former enemies.

Another formation for a drill begins when the riders have split into two lines. One line trots up one side of the ring, the other line up the opposite side. At the top corners, both leaders begin to take a diagonal path to their opposite corner. The lines will cross in the center of the ring, one partner of each pair passing in front of the other en route.

A wheel makes an impressive formation. Begin by having the riders learn how to reverse with four horses together in a row. The inside horse turns slowly, the outside horse may need to canter. If you have eight horses to form a wheel, four horses in a row face and move in one direction, four horses the opposite way, all eight in a straight line.

One summer I watched a drill team of 16 horses at a summer camp. Not only did they turn a wheel in both directions, they set up a row of jumps across the field and jumped together.

The children enjoy jumping in pairs or four together. Their timing needs to be exact and their ability should be about equal.

If you add a buggy to your equipment, all of your riders will want to learn to drive. You will find, no doubt, several horses in your stable which have been in harness before. Keep the buggy in a ring, or a safe area, free of traffic, while your riders are using it.

One day that all your riders will enjoy is the day of a gymkhana. Draw up a list of games that can be played on horseback. Some games are just for fun, some are devised to show a rider's skill. You will be able to use a few of the games the children have played in classes.

A relay race carrying cups of water is a successful game for a gymkhana. Each child on the team is given a cup full of water. One girl walks around the ring carrying

All of your riders will want to know how to drive if you own a buggy.

her cup, the next girl trots around the ring, the next canters, and the final one rides bareback at any gait she chooses. The team with the most water left in their cups is the winner.

Another game the children enjoy involves placing a piece of paper under the knee of each child who is entered for the game. While walking, trotting and cantering, the child who loses her paper last is the winner.

A costume race is fun for the spectators. Put a large-sized blouse and pants in a paper bag. Each child on a team rides to the end of the field where the bag lies and puts on the blouse and pants over her riding clothes. She returns to the next rider to whom she gives the costume. The team which completes the changes of clothes and finishes first wins.

An egg and spoon race, using potatoes instead of eggs, works well. Obstacle races with a gate, a log, two poles between which the horse must back without touching either one, a low jump, are easy to plan. Walking races are quite safe and easy to judge.

If you plan a gymkhana carefully and pick the riders for each class with certainty that the class is not too difficult for anyone, it will be a happy day.

The idea behind trail rides, games in the woods, and bareback riding, is teaching proficiency under all circumstances. Every event you plan should be considered from the point of view of safety first. The more excited riders become, the less cautious they become. If your planning has been successful, all of your riders will share happiness with your horses.

14

WAYS TO TACKLE FEAR AND DISABILITY

In any group of children a few present problems for an instructor. The common problem is fear, often hidden or disguised. Then there are children who are overweight or have physical handicaps. With patience they can all be taught to be good riders. Just because these children do take more time than others in the class, you may find it necessary to give them shorter lessons. But, the individual instruction is more valuable than an extra 15 minutes or so on a horse.

You will recognize the frightened child on her first day of riding. Some children will get over their fear easily after patting the horse and discovering he is not so big after all. Most children cease to be afraid after they have trotted the first time, because they learn they are able to stay on the horse.

The child who worries you is the one who is deeply afraid. The moment you touch such a child you feel how tense she is. Even if she controls her smile, a really frightened child's leg will tremble when she takes the trotting position. You know she is one child who must not trot by herself for a while. Even when you let her walk, have an assistant walk beside her. The assistant is there to give her confidence. If a frightened child slips to one side of her saddle, or bumps into the horse ahead because she cannot stop her horse, even though she is unhurt, she may be so frightened she will not ride again.

When I wanted a picture of a frightened child, the instructors at one camp volunteered a six-year-old. As soon as I focused the camera, the child gave me the happiest smile I had seen all day. The opportunity to give her a little encouragement was too good to miss, so I told her I needed a picture of a frightened child trotting. "Oh, I can trot," the child said at once. And she did. Just that bit of encouragement got her over being afraid.

Another child refused to admit her fear and won the hearts of the instructors with her courage. She was a roly-poly blond who shook so hard when she stood in her trotting position, her pants quivered. In spite of her fear, because of her desire to learn to ride, she never missed a lesson. She was assigned to Juli, a quiet-spoken, encouraging type of counsellor. It took the child nearly two weeks to learn to post. When she finally felt the rhythm, her face lit with a smile that glowed for every instructor in the department. Although she remained tense for many days, her pride in accomplishment was so great it conquered her fear.

There are several ways to help a frightened child. One is to allow her to ride the same horse every day. The horse should be absolutely reliable, one who will never hurry, one who will trot easily, one she can trust. A small horse or pony is less fearsome to a rider than is a larger horse. Always send someone with the child until she is willing to go alone and is capable of controlling her horse without assistance. If you can keep her in line with the other children, she will make every effort to be like them, to ride alone as soon as she dares to, and to stay on the full hour.

Do not build up the fact that she is afraid, or make her feel the problem can persist. The method of instruction is the same as for any other child. Unless the child is so frightened that it is impossible to get her to trot, she should be encouraged to do so in her first lesson. The

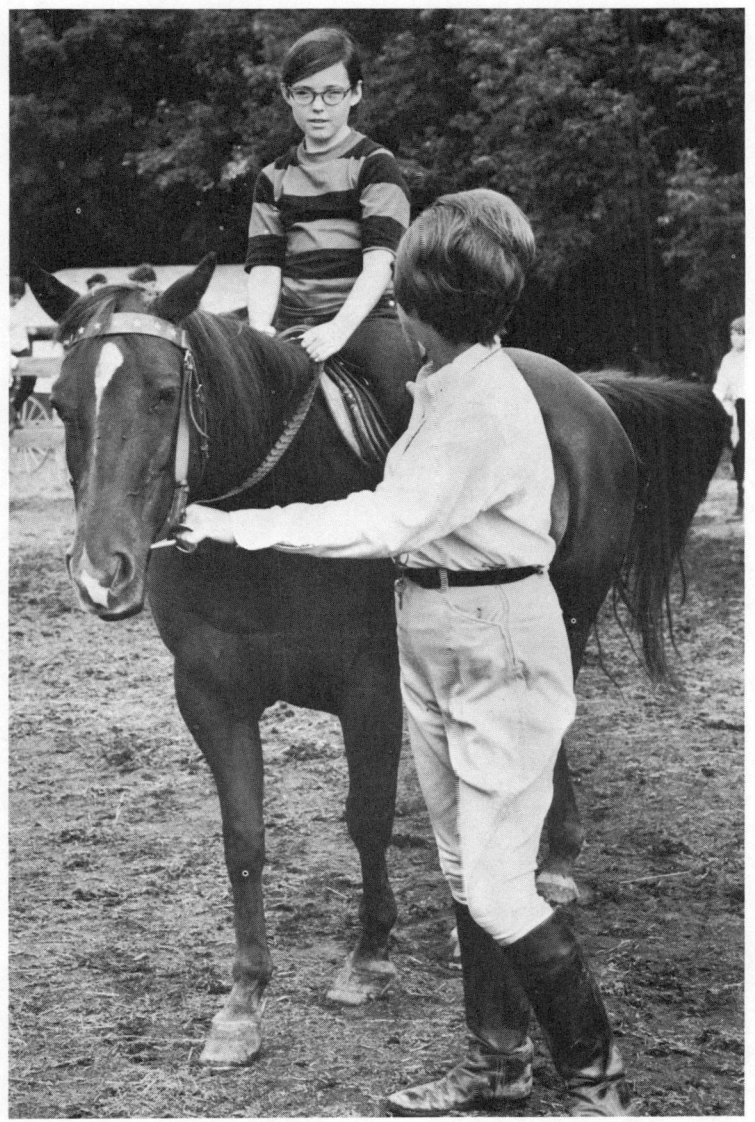

A small horse is less fearsome for the frightened child to ride than a big one is.

The instructor should hold the child's arm and leg while someone else leads the horse.

Ways to Tackle Fear and Disability

fact that she can trot safely will do a great deal to overcome her fear. The first few times she trots have one instructor hold her by her arm and her leg while another instructor or a child leads the horse. This is a sure way to have control of the horse, both to make him trot and to stop. The child feels secure because she is being held firmly. You do not worry that some incident will occur to the horse to increase the child's fear.

Even when the child is willing to trot by herself, send someone along beside her in case she needs a helping hand. Urge the child to try to do more, but never force her to do something when she is afraid. If you are patient and kind, the child will conquer her fear and learn to ride.

Sometimes fear is disguised with bravado in older children. Take care to give such a child the same encouragement and praise you give children who have more pleasing attitudes.

The most difficult case of fear to conquer is fear that has been induced by an accident with a horse. The best cure is a great deal of riding. Horses themselves will restore a child's confidence.

If such a child comes to you for lessons, even if she has the skills of an advanced rider, be extremely careful that she is given gentle horses to ride. The worst thing that can happen to her is another accident on a horse. Although a child's knowledge may be sufficient to ride advanced horses, her fear will be communicated to the horse so that he does not quite trust his rider. In an emergency, her fear often is so great she takes the wrong action.

Among your advanced horses should be one or two that are quiet enough for a two-year-old child, yet well enough trained to appeal to good riders. Tiny Tim was a horse of that type. He was a large black horse, an excellent jumper, responsive to aids, but never made a mistake.

If the earth opened to a chasm in front of his nose, I am sure he would have stood still and waited expectantly for it to close again. This is the type of horse to use with riders who have been frightened by horses in the past.

The child's desire to ride again is the biggest asset she brings to lessons. Your encouragement will increase this desire. The more knowledge you can give her, the safer she will be and the faster her confidence will grow.

Frequently, the child's love for a single horse will help her conquer her fear. Allow her to ride this horse as often as she likes. He may do for her what it would take you months to accomplish.

My son was six before he had an accident with a horse. He mounted a big black mare, Twilight, before a horse show. The mare was never used in horse shows because she had a terror for waving papers, and programs in the hands of spectators were always being waved. Sure enough, he had hardly started to walk before a program blew past her. As she darted around the ring, she dumped him in the mud. Even though he had not been hurt, his enthusiasm for riding dropped sharply. The fear could be detected under the surface for two or three years. White Stripe was his cure. No one understood why he loved the horse. White Stripe was old, ugly, had terrible gaits, and would on occasion jump over the side of the ring. Only to my son, was White Stripe wonderful. A year later White Stripe died. The hardest thing I ever had to do was to tell my son; but before he died, White Stripe had given my son a great gift: confidence. This made him a rider.

Even teenagers learn to overcome fear if you find the right horse. Karen, who was an advanced rider, was so tense with fear she could turn a quiet horse into a demon almost as soon as she mounted. Although the instructor continued to give Karen the quietest horses she had in the barn, Karen liked none of them. Which horse did Karen want to ride? The most difficult horse in the stable to

Ways to Tackle Fear and Disability

control. Karen was a determined girl. She persuaded her parents to buy the horse. Her love for the horse won the victory over her fear. A year later she could ride him anywhere.

The problem of overweight is often as much a mental difficulty as fear is. Excessive weight does not prevent a child from learning to ride well. Because weight interferes with the child's accomplishments in so many sports, she *thinks* it will prevent her from riding.

Actually, only two phases of riding may be difficult for her. One is mounting, the other is posting. Until she learns how to mount easily, use a mounting block or give her a leg up. After she acquires balance on the horse, she will be able to mount without assistance.

In spite of being overweight, many children are able to balance in their trotting position the first day. You need to be certain of their balance, however, before allowing them to post. They must be able to sit down lightly on the saddle, not slump into it. This does not have to be difficult. Their legs will support them if they keep their heels down and their legs under their bodies in the correct position.

Once the heavy child has learned to post, all other riding skills should be as easy for her to acquire as they are for anyone else. She can become skilled at all gaits and even jump well.

The instructor can do much to make riding easier for the overweight child. The problems of weight should be recognized and the child shown how to cope with them, but the instructor should nip any sense of discouragement the instant it appears. Only encouragement and treating the girl the same as every other child in the class will help her.

Many physical handicaps do not interfere with a child's riding. Riders with trick knees, weak ankles, inflexible joints, a leg that will not support weight—all have been

The heavy child can become a skilled rider.

taught to ride in safety. Each problem must be dealt with on an individual basis. A mental block about her disability often increases the difficulty of handling a child with a problem. It is most important not to pamper the individual. Do not allow whining, defeatism, or stubbornness to affect your own disposition or win a sympathetic response from you.

The child may need more encouragement than the others in the class do. However, make certain praise is merited, because it is not always given honestly to a handicapped child. You need her trust most of all and praise at the right moments will help you win it.

A child with a bad leg can be mounted on the right if you choose a horse who will tolerate an approach from the right side. Teach the importance of balance, not grip. Even if a child is unable to flex her ankle, she will be

Ways to Tackle Fear and Disability

secure if she learns to keep her thigh against the saddle by means of outward pressure on her heel.

Sometimes you need to compromise on a child's position. A handicapped child may post awkwardly, but if she gets the rhythm and uses the upward thrust of the horse to post, she will be able to trot.

Always use a reliable horse with handicapped children, no matter to which ring they are assigned. They are more susceptible to hurt and must be protected in every way possible. Have an instructor go beside the horse of the handicapped child until her control is excellent.

Whatever the problem you face with a child, if you will keep your poise and confidence, your smile and soft voice, with the horse's help and the rider's cooperation, you can beat the problem.

15

SAFETY IN THE SADDLE

Children can think of the strangest things to do around horses. If only one could predict what they would think of next! Inexperienced riders, grown to adulthood, often do foolish things themselves. Every instructor adopts certain rules that must be obeyed around his horses. If you explain why something is dangerous, most riders will avoid it without reminders. Most accidents occur because someone did not know his action could cause an accident.

My own list of pet peeves is not really long, but if a child is caught doing one of them my temper is short, not because I am angry with the child but because I am afraid for her. No one wants a child to be hurt. Safety in the ring is one of the best forms of advertising you can have, because parents realize you are taking care of those they love most in the world. The fact that lawsuits are something to be avoided is an added incentive to safe riding.

When a group of riders are together, their safety depends to a large extent on how well they listen and the distance they keep from each other. Because an instructor is able to detect something wrong moments before an inexperienced rider does, the instructor can prevent the accident if the class is listening to her and obeys instantly. From the first day of riding, classes should be drilled in instant obedience to any command. The commands should begin with "ALL STOP" and include emergency dismounts, shortening reins, grabbing the mane, leaning back, and

Children think of the craziest things to do on horses.

Riders should be conscious of the importance of keeping a safe distance away from other horses.

any other command the instructor makes. Children should learn to obey without asking why. The reason will be evident to them all too quickly.

The importance of keeping four or five feet away from the nearest horse needs to be impressed on all riders. This is especially true on trail rides, because the class is happy to be free and everyone forgets half of what you have taught. Children tend to think ring rules are not trail rules. It is especially important for children to keep their horses apart in the stableyard, because the danger of a friend being kicked is even greater when a child is on the ground than on a horse. Horses do not cooperate with their riders about keeping a proper distance from their stablemates. This makes it more difficult to keep them far enough away from each other to prevent kicking and biting.

There are right ways and wrong ways to act around horses. A basic rule is to be quiet and calm. Horses, like all animals, want their lives arranged according to a routine. Anything that varies from the normal, or happens unexpectedly, worries or frightens them.

So many simple objects can startle a horse: a waving paper, a sweater flying onto the fence post as the rider tries to discard it in the heat of the day, a jacket that has been tied around a girl's waist that suddenly drops to the ground, a rock the instructor throws out of the ring into the grass. Any one of these sudden motions can cause a horse to shy or bolt.

A horse is startled, much as a person is, by being hit unexpectedly. One riding instructor, known among her friends as "Pretty Blue" because of the lovely shades of blue she often wore, had a distaste for being touched unexpectedly. She jumped and gave a yell if a child came up behind her and touched her arm. A horse will jump, too, if he is smacked on the croup, or slapped on the neck without any warning. Often a horse that is well-mannered will kick or bite if he is hit by someone he cannot see. Some-

Safety in the Saddle

times children are being friendly when they hit a horse on the croup as they pass by him. Sometimes when putting a horse into a pasture or a stall, a child gives a final swat just to see him kick up his heels or to hurry him on his way. A horse should not be hit anywhere by a rider when the rider is on foot.

Children outside the ring can unwittingly cause an accident by the way they act. Although there is not a horse within a dozen feet of them, when children "rough-house," race around and shout, a horse in the ring may see the sudden movement and be frightened. One of the worst things a child can do is to scream. Horses' ears are extremely sensitive. Neither in play nor in fear should a child scream. A scream also frightens every instructor. If children are taught to walk quietly and to talk quietly in the stable area, they may also remember to keep calm even in an emergency when riding a horse.

No matter how confident a child may be about a horse's disposition, she should not give him a reason to mistrust her when she is around him. When she is cleaning him or fastening his girth, she should not go under his belly, not even duck underneath his neck. Without intending to hurt her, he might lift his foot and his hoof is big and hard wherever it hits you. If he ducks his chin to bite his shoulder when a child is going beneath a horse's neck, he can knock her head.

Even when it comes to feeding a horse, rules need to be established. The best rule is to allow no hand feeding at all. Treats of carrots and apples can be added to grain rations. However, if a child does feed her horse, her fingers should lie flat, her palm open, so he does not bite her fingers instead of the treat.

Adults, too, need to understand their responsibilities around horses. Smoking should never be allowed in a stable area. There are too many inflammable items around, from hay and straw to fences and barns.

The way children act on horses determines their safety

A rider should not stick her fingers in front of a horse's mouth to feed him.

Safety in the Saddle

as much as their behavior on the ground. Of all the things children do, the one that scares me most is seeing them lying down on their horses' backs. This is, I realize, a personal prejudice.

Years ago, when I was relaxing on Little Major, a horse I had been riding for two or three years and trusted implicitly, a riding instructor taught me a lesson. She thought it would be funny to see what Little Major would do if she scared him. So, she waved both hands at him suddenly. Little Major did more than jump. He leaped out from under me as if a bomb had gone off beneath his feet. I didn't go with him because I was lying down so comfortably. Later, when I was nursing a broken wrist, the riding instructor said miserably, "I knew better, really I did."

Of course, I knew who was really to blame: I was. Not only had I been lying down with my head pillowed on my horse's croup, but I did not even have a secure enough hold on the reins to keep control of my horse.

Sometimes it is difficult to convince children that they must have control of their horses at all times, which means holding the reins all of the time. *All of the time* includes when a child is fixing her stirrups, or tightening her girth from the saddle, or talking to her friend on the other side of the fence.

One morning, when the riding rings at camp had been going smoothly for weeks, the call "ALL STOP" was shouted from the beginners' ring. For some reason Steppy, who was usually such a good pony, had trotted fast to the end of the ring. A few minutes later, Steppy trotted off again. His rider was upset although she had not slipped off and Steppy had stopped properly when everyone else stopped. The next time an instructor in the advanced ring glanced across at the beginners' ring, she was shocked to see all the girls who were riding holding both hands in the air. A new instructor was giving the class exercises.

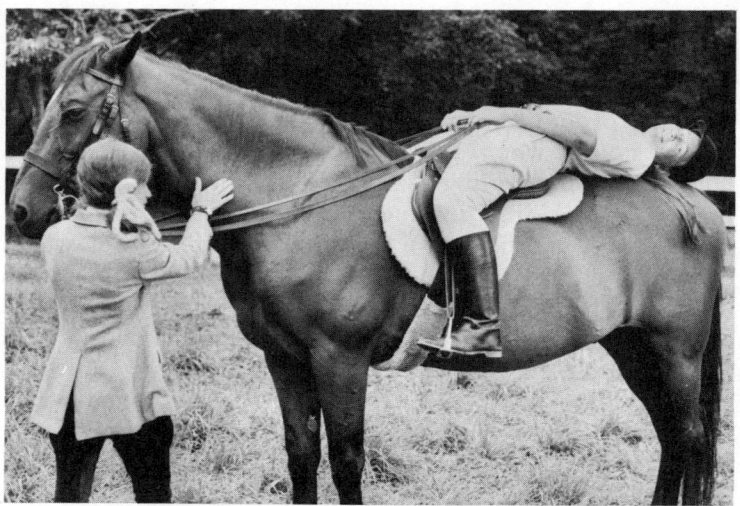

A rider flirts with danger if she lies down on a horse's back.

Poor Steppy, who expected someone to hold his reins and tell him when to stop, had been blamed for trotting right around the ring.

Because children like to ride bareback, it is often difficult to refuse to allow them to ride bareback on trail. When you are working with groups of children, you cannot give special attention to one or two who are bareback when the entire trail ride demands attention. Most children feel more secure with saddles; trail is the place to use them. So many unexpected incidents occur while you are on trail. Horses shy at strange objects; people pop out at odd moments. If a child is on a saddle when her horse is startled, she has something to hang on to with her legs and hands, whether what she grabs fits into proper riding form or not.

It is proper form for an inexperienced rider to keep her heels down, but it is also very important for her safety.

Safety in the Saddle

A foot should not be shoved home in the stirrup.

When a child shoves her foot home in the stirrup, which usually happens when her heels go up, her foot will not slip out of the stirrup easily. If she is thrown or slips off the saddle, she could be dragged by her foot sticking in the stirrup.

A child can also be dragged by the leather strap of her riding crop, if she wears the looped strap over her wrist. The crop can catch on the saddle or behind a stirrup leather as a child slips to the ground. Those nice loops the manufacturers put on riding crops should not be used to hold them.

High on the list of unsafe things to do on a horse is riding double. One girl or the other will not have a secure grip. The extra rider, moreover, interferes with the control of the rider who is holding the reins. If the unexpected happens, each child increases the chance of the other one being hurt.

Children are surprised to be told it is unsafe to chew gum while riding. When you are teaching jumping, you should check your class to be certain no one has gum in her mouth. A sudden jar, which occurs frequently when children are learning to ride, could cause a child to swallow her gum and choke on it.

There are rules for safety that apply to riding apparel. Many stables insist that all riders wear correct riding habits, from boots to hard hats, whenever they ride. The reason is not so much to make the riders appear smart as it is to make them safe. Riding boots have leather soles which slip out of stirrups easily in emergencies. Riding breeches and jodhpurs cover the rider's legs so that she is not hurt by stirrup leathers or rubbing her legs against a horse's sides. Hard hats should have elastic straps beneath the riders' chins so that the hats stay on even if the riders are jarred.

It is important that riders wear hard hats when jumping. A fall that occurs when a child is going over a jump brings

No one should go barefoot around horses.

her in closer contact with a horse's heels than she might come at another time. Although your jumping system is safe, safer in most phases than teaching cantering or going on trail, children need to learn habits of safety, and jumping is potentially one of the most dangerous parts of riding.

Children should not go barefoot around horses. Horses are heavy animals; both horses and children are careless. Although it may seem to a child that her horse stepped on her deliberately, it was just an accident. If she is barefoot or wearing sneakers or thronged shoes or sandals, she is going to be hurt more than if she is wearing leather shoes or riding boots.

If a child does not own riding boots, she should wear leather soled shoes that tie when she is riding. Other shoes do not slip out of the stirrup easily and some slip off her heel continuously.

Riding instructors should obey every rule of safety established for the riders. Children learn much more by example than adults like to admit. Bad habits seem almost contagious.

Since you cannot control all the features of riding all of the time, you need to be rigid about safety rules which control some of the features some of the time.

16

HORSE SHOW

The crowning joy of being able to ride, to most children, is being in a horse show. They will anticipate the day for weeks, work for it with genuine effort, and come dressed that day in their finest riding apparel. The decisions of the judges will be regarded sacred and final, setting the blue ribbon winners on a pedestal of glory.

To you, a horse show is one of the hardest days of work you put into a riding program. The better your preparation, the more quickly and smoothly the show will go, and the easier the day will be.

Since it is necessary to bring this type of happiness to your riders, make the most of it with good advance publicity. Newspapers in the local community, as well as those in other areas from which some of your clientele come, should be notified of the date. The names of the winners in each class should be sent to the papers after the horse show. As part of your publicity, print or mimeograph programs so that each child, as well as every spectator may have his own.

The show will seem more professional if you have a public address system. Everyone at the show, not just the children involved, want to know who won in a class. It is difficult to make these announcements loud enough for everyone to hear unless you have a P.A. system. The next best substitute is an electric megaphone. If you are unable to have either of these, be sure the person who announces

The judge is ready; the class has been called; and you know she is thinking, "I may win."

Horse Show

the winners has silence from the audience and is standing elevated above the crowd to give everyone the best chance to hear.

Line up your judges well in advance, not a few days before your show. Choose judges who are in sympathy with the way you teach riding. Children need an "understanding" judge, one who has the ability to discern when the horse is at fault and not the child, one who will speak to the children afterward to ease the bitterness of those who lost and praise the winners.

You need to order ribbons for the horse show in advance. If you do not order early, the company will be unable to print your name on the ribbons and you lose the publicity value that ribbons continue to give you for years while they hang in some child's room. Divide the ribbons before the show and hang a set for each class on a hanger. Be sure to have a few extra for ties. If it is possible to have ribbons for everyone, even if some are only "entrance ribbons," it means much happiness for children. A trophy, even an inexpensive one, for the top rider in beginners, intermediates, and advanced will be long treasured.

As soon as the day for the horse show is set, the children will want to know in which class they are going to ride and how the horses are to be assigned. This involves paper work for you.

First, you need to divide your horses. Begin by eliminating every horse that is likely to be spooky or excitable in a show-ring with a crowd of people around. Next, decide which horses you will use for the beginners, intermediates and advanced. The number of horses you feel are safe for each group determines the size of your classes in each. You may use the same horses in every group. If you do, you can only operate a single ring at a time on the day of the horse show. If the horses are divided into two or more groups, however, you will be able to operate two rings at once.

Next, divide your riders into groups on the basis of ability. The fairer your divisions are, the fairer the classes will be. Some children will surprise you and ride beyond their ability, others will go to pieces during the horse show, so do not sweat over the borderline cases when you are making up classes.

Finally, make a set of lots with numbers for the children to draw. Only one class draws numbers at a time. If you have 12 horses in one beginners' class, have 12 numbers; call the 12 children who are to ride and have each draw a number. Whoever draws number one has first choice of horses. The child with number 12 will be unhappy that she has last choice, but she will not complain that you were unfair about assigning horses. Be sure you have a list of horses in plain view during the drawing to save you from answering questions. Be patient during the drawing process. It will be difficult, but keep smiling.

As soon as the drawing is finished, post a list of classes with the horses each child is to ride. This, too, saves a multitude of questions. On the list each child should have a number, the number she will wear during the horse show. These numbers can also be ordered before the show, or you can make your own. Be sure the numbers are large enough and dark enough for the judge to see easily. The numbers should be fastened securely on the backs of the riders.

The horse show will go much more smoothly if you rehearse the classes the day before. This has the added advantage of giving each rider an opportunity to ride the horse she will ride during the show. Try to make your riders realize that in a horse show the winners are not always the best riders nor the losers the worst. A judge has no way of knowing which horses are the easiest to ride, which ones the most difficult.

I remember telling a judge, who was a friend, that Pixie was one of the most willing horses in the stable, and to try to take this into account when she judged. She did try. Yet after the show, as I glanced down the program at the winners, Pixie's rider had taken a ribbon in every class. How can a judge be sure how much credit for a fine display of horsemanship should go to the rider and how much to the horse?

Explain to your riders that sometimes a judge happens to glance at a good rider when she makes a mistake, but fails to notice when someone else does something wrong. Judges do not have eyes in the back of their heads. Some people do not ride well under pressure; others shine when riding before an audience. The rider who relaxes as she rides in a show will have a better chance of winning than the tense rider who becomes stiff in her effort to look well. The practice show will help the tense riders to have a little more confidence on the big day.

The instructors should act as judges for the mock horse show. The riders from one class may also help judge another. This often shows them how a judge judges a show better than anything you can say. Announce the winners in the practice show, although you do not give ribbons. After each class, the instructors should go over their written lists with the riders to show everyone her mistakes and strong points.

Recently, I was given the score sheets a group of counsellors made while judging a practice horse show. In the beginners' classes, which had been judged only at a walk, a trot and stopping, the most common fault was riding with heels up. The next most frequent mistake involved children who hunched forward over their horses and those whose toes pointed straight out. A few children let their legs slip forward or looked down while they rode. The winners were the children who remembered to keep their heels down and could stop their horses easily.

Among the intermediates, were the faults different? No, heels that went up and children who leaned forward when trotting or stopping placed the lowest in their classes. These faults were always coupled with difficulty in control. A child who forgot to change diagonals never placed first.

In the advanced classes the emphasis changed to control. The girl who could make her horse canter without falling backward in the process, who could keep him trotting when he was circling, who could make him jump and stop, was always the winner. If a child forgot to change diagonals or failed to take the correct lead, she did not win top honors.

One of the most noticeable faults among the advanced group was toes that stuck out at right angles to the horse. Because an instructor usually watches a child from the side when she is teaching jumping, she does not always notice and correct this fault. When a child sticks out her

It is not so important how the rider does it, but that she gets him over the jump.

Horse Show

toes while she is jumping she automatically loosens her legs against her horse. I happened to take a picture of Sarah as she was going over a jump one day. Sarah always had a perfect galloping position whenever you looked at her, but the picture showed that while she was jumping her toes went out just as she cleared the bar. After a horse show in which she had placed last in her class, Sarah asked me what she had been doing wrong. I told her what the picture had shown. Sarah worked on those toes, and therefore on her leg position, for four weeks. In the next horse show, riding with the same girls, she won the championship.

On the day of the horse show, have each instructor responsible for one or two classes. She should make sure that all of the riders for her classes are waiting at the gate before the classes are called. Each child should have her number on, and her hair should be out of the way. As each child mounts, she should make sure her stirrups are even and the correct length. Sissy, a camper I liked because she always smiled when things went wrong and was always ready to help the other campers, only showed her disappointment in her eyes when she lost in a horse show. As she rode toward me, I knew immediately why she had lost. One of her stirrups was at least two holes shorter than the other and much too short for her.

Before the class starts, the instructor should give the riders a few words of encouragement. A class of children will be so excited you would think it was Christmas morning. The bit of encouragement will calm most of the girls slightly.

The first classes in the horse show should be the beginners, the final ones the advanced jumpers. While one class is being judged, the next class should be gathered by the gate, ready to spring onto the horses as soon as the other riders have dismounted. If you only have one judge, but two rings, two sets of children may be mounted

Uneven stirrups will prevent a rider from winning. Whoever helps mount the class should be sure stirrups are correctly adjusted.

Horse Show

at once; the second set is then ready to ride as soon as the judge comes into the ring. The top classes, the most advanced ones, should have the limelight all to themselves. No other class should ride at the time they do.

You may wish to begin the horse show with an exhibition ride by your varsity team. Keep the formations they use well within the range of their ability. You become quite embarrassed if the riders on display cannot reverse together, for example, when half-a-hundred people are watching them try. Make sure they are ready to ride about half an hour before the show is scheduled to begin. Otherwise, the judge is there waiting to work, the spectators are impatient because they arrived early, and all the riders are milling around underfoot.

Flags are impressive when carried by horses. As the horses canter around the ring, there is no doubt in the minds of the spectators that the show is about to begin. The riders charged with the responsibility of carrying the waving emblems of their country have pride written all over them.

Take care who carries the flag if you use one. Take even greater care that the rings nearby have no mounted riders. The worst bedlam I remember at a horse show was caused by two flags. One was red with the emblem of the camp sewn in the center. If it had been the cape of a toreador and the adjoining ring filled with bulls rather than horses, it could have not started the animals charging any faster. As the flag passed the ring where a group of beginners were mounted, the horses scattered to the far end of the ring. At that moment, the flag reversed and came waving toward them again. A second charge occurred. Amazingly enough, no child fell off. I would have given every mounted rider a blue ribbon right then and there, had I had my way.

One of the instructors should act as a ringmaster during the horse show. She will be able to give commands to the children in a form they understand. This is particularly important in the beginners' ring because the inexperienced riders need the reassurance of the familiar. Use a lead horse for the beginners just as you do during lessons. Give the riders a chance to walk and rest between periods of trotting.

In intermediate classes do not ask the riders to do everything they are capable of doing. Make the horse show just a bit easier than they expect. The classes will be safer and the children will look more experienced if everyone in the class is able to do everything the ringmaster asks them to do.

In jumping classes, do not set the jumps high. It is embarrassing for everyone if the horses refuse to jump. The children will be too excited to get the best out of their horses, so do not increase the difficulty for them.

The day of a horse show is not the day to relax rules. The riders should mount in the center of the ring. The ringmaster may need to remind them to hold their horses for the next riders. None of the riders should sit on the fence, even though the view is excellent. Not only may the fence break, the horses might disapprove. If sudden applause startles the horses, be ready to hold applause until the riders dismount.

At the end of each class, the horses should line up facing the spectators. Even in the beginners' ring, the horses in the line can be turned so their heads are toward the audience. The parents are usually just as proud as their children are of a ribbon, and it is wise to allow a few minutes for picture-taking if necessary.

The riders who did not win are often disconsolate. They make you wish everyone could win in a horse show. Since this is impossible, the riders need to learn the most valuable lesson the day can teach, sportsmanship. The way you speak to these children will make it easier for them to use the lesson as a stepping-stone to better riding.

Keep the jumps low. She needs all the help you can give.

The big moment: the riders line up facing the spectators.

The look you will get as the judge, ribbon in hand, comes forward to pin the rider.

Horse Show

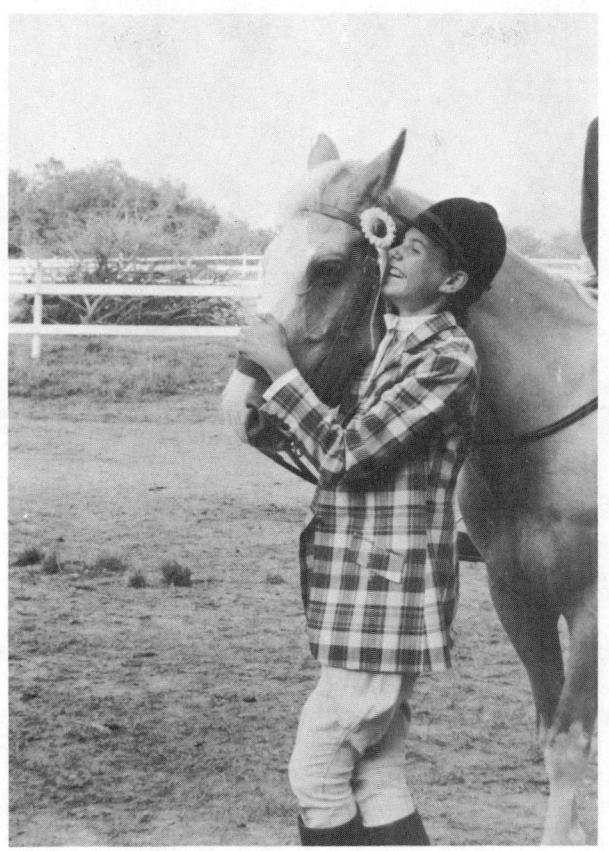

If you have taught her with fun and laughter, her joy will go deep and include you.

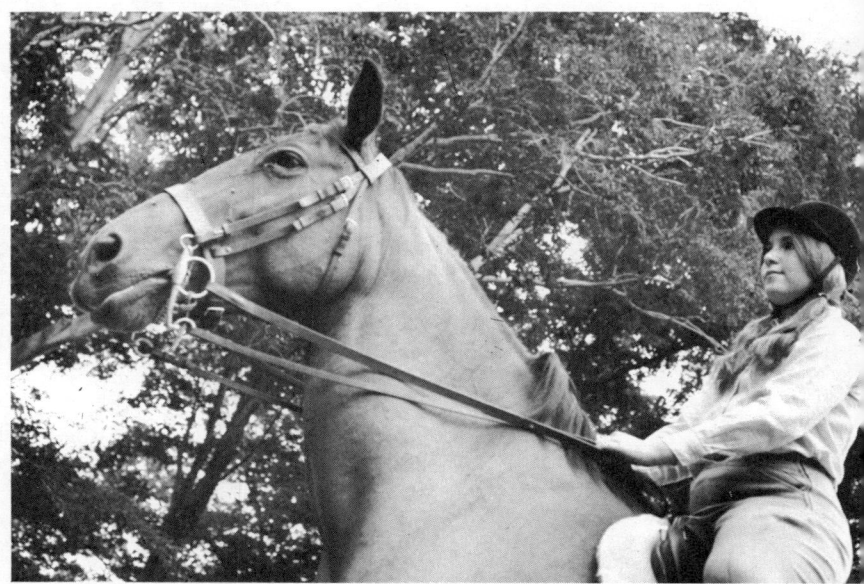

A great gift: to have happiness with horses, to catch the inspiration of the moment wherever she rides.

The horse show completes a riding program in a final way. When it is over, you have given your riders experience in the type of riding that is popular all over the country. They should be able to ride anywhere cross-country, take part in overnight rides, and enter horse shows with a degree of confidence that will make you proud. They will also know how to have pleasure with horses. This is, perhaps, your greatest gift to them.

INDEX

Ankles flexed, 52, 53, 154, 181, 196, 254
Arch(ing), 52, 54, 56, 68

Backing, 97, 145, 220
    controlled backing, 220
Balance, 45, 46, 49, 56, 61, 65, 79, 115, 152, 153, 236, 253, 254
    for dismounting, 80, 83, 86, 87
    for jumping, 183, 193, 196
    for mounting, 89
    mane for balance, 45
    off balance, 39, 56, 58, 107, 173, 181, 187, 190, 214, 225, 240
Bareback, 103, 232, 239, 240, 241, 246, 262
Barefoot, 265, 266
Bight of the reins, 39, 80, 158, 159
Bounce, 52, 115, 155, 173, 212
    double bounce, 65
Buck, 107
Buggy, 244, 245

Canter, 100, 104, 169–179, 187, 240
    figure eight at a canter, 220
    sit to the canter, 173, 174, 177, 272
Change of direction, 116, 117
Check girth, 89, 90, 181
Circles, 97, 104, 116, 190, 219, 222, 236, 272
Collect horse, 202
Common faults, 271
Confidence, 27, 33, 47, 51, 97
Control, 50, 79, 80, 86, 94, 104–121, 145, 158, 169, 173, 178, 181, 193, 196, 202, 210, 225, 272
Cool horses, 61
Coordination, 89
Courtesy, 122, 225
Crop, 105, 172, 191, 198
Crossing the street, 234
Crossing water, 234
Cut corners, 107

Determination, 97, 172, 197, 263
Diagonals, 104, 114, 115, 117, 219, 220, 236, 272
Disability, 247, 253, 254, 255
Dismounting, 59, 79–89, 119, 120, 233
Distance between horses, 33, 34, 122, 170, 233, 256–258
Divide classes, 269, 270
Double riding, 264
Draw lots for classes in horse show, 270
Drill, 117, 240, 242, 243, 244, 275

Elbows, 39, 60, 65, 75, 83, 109, 151, 162, 163
Emergency dismount, 59, 60–63, 65, 119, 217–219
Eyes, 46, 109, 183, 184, 186, 187, 220, 271

Face front, 60, 63, 83, 84, 95
Face rear, 92, 93
Fear prevented, 46, 47, 50, 59, 86, 247–252
Feeding tidbits, 259, 260
Feet, 27, 56, 61, 73, 82, 153, 187
    ball of foot, 43
    feet out of stirrups, 59, 60, 83, 87

feet shoved home, 43, 44, 52, 263, 264
position of feet, 65
sore foot, 103

Gallop, 223, 225
Galloping position, 45, 181–183, 185–187, 189, 193, 194, 196, 206, 223, 225, 273
Games, 99, 104–121, 179
    Come Over, 119
    Egg and Spoon Race, 246
    Follow the Leader, 151
    Hunt Day, 237, 238
    Mock Jumping, 119
    Musical Chairs, 118, 120, 240
    Paper under the Knees, 246
    Pig, 99, 100
    Races, 119
    Red Light, 165, 166
    Snatch the Bacon, 120, 121, 240
    Stirrup Tag, 239, 240
    Touch Every Fence Post, 151
    Virginia Reel, 118, 119
    War, 225
    Water Race, 244, 246
Girth, 130–132, 142–144
Grip, 153, 187, 254
Gum, 264
Gymkhana, 244, 246

Half seat, 45
Hands, 27, 28, 34–43, 45, 50, 68, 160–162, 207, 213
    at canter, 177
    close together, 45
    good hands, 150, 155, 164, 166, 207
    in air, 39, 75, 109, 261
    jumping, 202, 205–207
    on horse's neck, 68
    right side up, 50
    while dismounting, 80–83 86
    while mounting, 90, 92
Hard hat, 188, 264
Head position, 46, 107–109, 183, 187
Heels, 29, 31, 32, 43, 44, 50, 52, 105–107, 153, 154, 172, 181, 187, 191, 208, 225, 255, 262, 271
Holding the mane, 29, 33, 38, 45, 46, 64, 65, 172, 240, 241
    at canter, 174
    jumping, 187
    while dismounting, 80
    while mounting, 89
Holding the saddle, 68, 92, 93
    incorrectly, 83, 86, 95, 98
Horse show, 267–280
    flags, 275
    line-up, 276, 277
    numbers, 270
    rehearsal, 270, 271
    ribbons, 269, 276, 278
Horses kicking, 33, 122, 258
Horses, right characteristics for teaching, 14, 15, 18
How hard to work horses, 61
How to buy horses, 14, 15
Hunchers, 56, 271

Iceland ponies, 88, 141

Jump(ing), 45, 105, 169, 180–213, 230, 244, 272, 273
    hitting the saddle, 189, 190
    position, 180–183, 185
    rushing, 193
    timing, 194–198, 207, 244
    with your horse, 194
Jumps
    brush, 208
    chicken coop, 210, 211
    in and out, 198–202
    in horse show, 276, 277
    outside course, 211, 212
    solid, 210
    spread, 208, 209
Judge(s), 268–271, 275, 278

Index

Kick, 29, 31, 52, 104, 105, 106, 189, 191
  incorrectly, 83, 86, 95, 111
Knees, 50, 101, 103, 151, 154, 187
  bent, 46, 47, 65, 153
  flexed, 196
  touching horse, 83, 273
  touching saddle, 83, 208
Knock down, 191–193, 197

Lead(s), 175–177, 220–222, 236
Lead horse, 26, 33, 34, 50, 59, 117, 172, 236, 276
Leading a horse, 122–126, 229, 230, 250
Leaning too far forward, 73, 74, 271
Legs
  in dismounting, 82, 89
  in mounting, 94
  leg pressure, 104, 105, 107–109, 171, 172, 175, 191, 198, 217
  position, 50, 56, 151, 177, 181, 187, 271, 273
  stiff, 196
  still, 65, 73
  swinging, 56, 58, 68, 153
Leg up, 100–103, 122, 241, 242

Mounting, 27, 28, 59, 80, 89–103, 119, 122, 126, 135, 233, 241, 242, 253

Natural rider, 51
Need for a system, 21, 22, 24
Nipping, 96, 97, 258

Overweight, 247, 253, 254

Pairs, 104, 242
Photographs, 24
Position, 52, 55, 56, 65, 68, 150, 173, 181, 208
Posting, 50, 104, 115, 214, 253
  at a walk, 65
  correctly, 65, 66, 155
  every other beat, 66
  incorrectly, 73, 75, 155
  learning to post, 61, 67–72
  ready to post, 65
  without stirrups, 215
Posture, 52, 54–57, 109, 151, 225
Practice off the horse, 52
Pull mane, 33
Pull or jerk on bit or mouth, 65, 73–75, 83, 163, 187, 206, 207, 236
Pumping, 68, 69

Rainy days, 118–120, 239, 240
Refusal, 187, 190
Reins, 27, 30, 33–41, 43, 45, 50, 198
  bridge, 202–204
  curb, 144, 145
  double, 144–146
  dropped, 83, 86
  how to hold or use, 39–41, 80, 81, 89, 90, 144, 255, 80, 81, 89, 90, 144, 155, 158, 171
  lengthen, 83, 86
  long, 39
  release, 105, 108
  shorten, 39, 45, 50, 59, 83, 97, 105, 107, 109, 114, 181, 188
  slack, 73, 157
  snaffle, 144, 145
  tight, 97, 158
  wrong way to hold or use, 42, 73, 75, 107–111, 156, 158, 162
Relaxing on a horse, 261, 262
Response from a horse, 79, 165, 166, 175, 213
Reverse, 111–114
Rhythm, 65, 67, 68, 75, 208, 255
Riding rings, 18–21, 79
Runaway horse, 177–179, 236
Run out on jump, 190, 202

Safety, 19, 23, 26, 29, 33, 46, 50,

59, 80, 89, 169, 176, 180, 183, 187, 192, 225, 229, 231–236, 238, 246, 251, 256–266, 276
Seat, 150, 151, 153, 155, 166
Serpentine, 116, 117
Shoulders, 46, 56, 68, 173
Sit down gently, 94, 103
Slip or fall off (prevention), 45–47, 49, 50, 56, 59, 240
Slouchers, 50, 225
Smoking around stable, 259
Standing up, 45, 46, 50, 52, 56, 65, 83, 115, 117, 180, 181
Stirrups
  adjust, 94, 130, 133–140, 149, 181
  correct, 153
  even, 273
  how to lengthen, 80, 91, 181
  run up, 147–149
  too long, 52, 95, 153
  too short, 52
  twisted leathers, 95, 135
  uneven, 274
  untwisted leathers, 141, 144
  without stirrups, 214, 215, 225
Stopping, 33, 34, 38, 39, 47, 59, 64, 65, 75, 80, 107, 108, 110, 126, 170, 177, 178, 236, 256, 261, 271
Stretch forelegs, 133
Stubborn horse, 104
Supple muscles, 79, 151, 214

Tack, 126–134
Teachers, qualifications, 13, 16, 21, 22, 24, 58
Teaching aids, 121, 122, 179, 194, 225, 246, 276. *See* Games
  at canter, 169
  Cooperation, 103, 255
  confidence, 255
  corrections, 56
  criticism, 151

division of classes, 79
encouragement, 172, 251, 253, 273
enthusiasm, 24, 25, 44
helpers, 89, 122, 123
patience, 247
photographs, 24
praise, 25, 56, 97, 151, 190, 254
reward and punishment, 189
stress the right, 22
trail, 231
trotting position, 45–58
use of ponies, 66, 88, 248, 249
Toe(s), 52, 73, 151, 153, 145, 181, 272
Trail rides, 18, 229–236, 238, 246, 258, 262
Trotting, 46, 52, 100, 104, 172, 186, 188
  alone, 51
  and posting, 65
  correct position, 73
  extended (fast) trot, 173,
  figure eight, 219
  how to, 105
  normal trot, 214
  practice, 61, 214
  ready to trot, 50
  slow trot, 152, 214, 216, 240
  three speeds of the trot, 214, 219
  with lead horse, 51
Trotting position, 45–58, 65, 66, 68, 71, 115, 151, 153, 181, 182–236
Turn, 30, 97, 104, 105, 109, 111, 112, 119, 163, 164, 190

Varsity, 242, 243, 275

Walk
  and emergency dismount, 61
  how to, 29, 31, 33

    in circle, 111
    in trotting position, 50
Weight
    on hands, 82, 83, 86
    on stirrups, 44, 46, 47, 224, 225
    use of, 105, 107–110, 130, 172, 181, 208, 236